1-10-11

Use The Diamond Touch!

Nate Booth

THE

DIAMOND TOUCH

*How to Get What You Want
by Giving People
What They
Uniquely
Desire*

"We use Dr. Nate Booth's services at Dow Chemical on a regular basis. His material is usable and powerful! Read The Diamond Touch *today to learn the skills that will take the quality of your relationships to the next level."*

RICK SCHAFFER
Director of Sales
Dow Chemical Company

"We use Nate Booth to teach the Diamond Touch to all our associates and agents. You need to learn what this man is teaching!"

ROGER LOOYENGA
Senior VP Marketing
Auto-Owners Insurance

"Nate Booth's Diamond Touch was embraced by our company because it was powerful and easy to put into practice."

IRENE CHASE
Director of Training
New England Restaurant Co., Inc.

"Nate's book will show how to get what you want most by giving people what they uniquely desire. This win-win thinking is a vital element of effective influence!"

CHRIS BROCK
Director of Advertising and Promotion, Mid-Atlantic States and Dixie Regions
REMAX

"You can't afford not to learn what Nate Booth is teaching. The concepts in The Diamond Touch *will make a huge difference in your life."*

MARY KOWALSKY
Vice President
Southwest Event Management
Bank of America

THE

DIAMOND TOUCH

*How to Get What You Want
by Giving People
What They
Uniquely
Desire*

DR. NATE BOOTH

NATE BOOTH & ASSOCIATES
Las Vegas

DEDICATION

In loving memory of my dad, Robert Booth,

a unique man who lived life to the fullest

and taught his children all the right lessons.

Nate Booth & Associates
1365 Fox Acres Drive
Las Vegas, NV 89134
Copyright © 1998 by Nate Booth

Designed by Robert Mott & Associates, www.Mottopia.com
Edited by Just Write Literary & Editorial Partners, www.JustWriteNow.com

Second printing 2005
2   3   4   5   6   7   8   9   10
ISBN 0-9649500-1-4

**ATTENTION CORPORATIONS, UNIVERSITIES, COLLEGES,
AND PROFESSIONAL ORGANIZATIONS:**
Quantity discounts are available on bulk purchases of this book
for educational or training purposes. Special books or book excerpts
can also be created to fit specific needs.
For information, please contact
Nate Booth & Associates
1365 Fox Acres Drive, Las Vegas, NV 89134 • (800) 917-0008
e-mail nbooth@NateBooth.com
www.NateBooth.com

CONTENTS

ACKNOWLEDGMENTS

There may be only one author of a book, but there are usually dozens of people who contribute to its quality. I would like to thank those people in my life. First of all, I would like to thank my wife, Dawn, and my daughter, Belinda, for putting up with my many hours in "the cave" creating this book. It's ironic that producing a book on relationships took me away from the people I love most for many hours.

I would also like to thank my #1 Associate at Nate Booth & Associates, Michael Crow. He is the epitome of spousehood and fatherhood and has given me many new insights into that slippery subject of human behavior.

As editors, the wonderful and talented Vicki St. George and her colleagues at Just Write wordsmithed my manuscript into a book that I believe you will find to be enjoyable to read and valuable to use.

I think you will agree that Robert Mott created a striking cover design and book layout that will energize your use of the book.

Finally, thank *you*. The average American reads less than one nonfiction book a year, and 58% of all Americans never read a nonfiction book after high school. You're one of "the few who do." Your curiosity and discipline will thrust you ahead in an era where the available knowledge in the world doubles every five years!

INTRODUCTION

The Power of Principles

MacGyver has just rescued the ambassador's daughter from the Colombian drug lords who were holding her captive. They have escaped to a small hut in the insect-infested jungle. The "bad guys" are closing in from all directions. The only "tools" MacGyver possesses are his trusty Swiss Army knife and a pack of chewing gum.

MacGyver notices the rearview mirror on an old Jeep in the yard outside the hut. He takes the mirror and creates a device that collects and concentrates sunlight, and then projects a concentrated ray of energy to the bad guys' Mercedes, blowing it up just in the nick of time. Then he builds a transmitter using his Swiss Army knife, chewing gum, and an ordinary radio. He calls his friends in Bogotá and is rescued by helicopter just before the next wave of bad guys appears.

If you've ever watched MacGyver on television, you know that I'm only slightly exaggerating. Even though the situation looks worse than hopeless, MacGyver always wins in the end. Why? Because MacGyver understands **the power of principles.** He understands the principles of physics, chemistry, and mechanics. This understanding gives MacGyver tremendous flexibility and power. He can be in any situation and use the resources around him to achieve his outcomes in life.

Principles allow you to create the best answer to almost every life question. Like MacGyver, when you apply the appropriate principles, you have the ability to be successful in a wide range of situations. This book is about helping you understand and use one of the most vital principles I know—something simple yet powerful that will enable you to create close relationships that prosper and last.

I call this principle **the Diamond Rule.** We're all familiar with the Golden Rule: "Do unto others as you would have them do unto you." In more modern language, "Treat people the way you'd like to be treated." But the Golden Rule has one shortcoming: **Everyone wants to be treated *differently*.** What may be excellent treatment to you may or may not be excellent treatment to others.

That's when the Diamond Rule comes into play. The Diamond Rule is, **"Treat others in the unique way *they* want to be treated."**

As you might imagine, the Diamond Rule is alive and well in all great relationships—husband/wife, parent/child, co-workers, service provider/customer, and salesperson/client. The purpose of this book is to assist you in thoroughly understanding the power of the Diamond Rule, and then applying the Rule to your unique set of life relationships.

In Section 1, you will discover what people really want in their lives. In Section 2, you will learn the questions you need to ask to discover what people really want in the key relationships of your life. In Section 3, you will learn how to quickly assess a person's desires, and in Section 4, you will discover what to do with the information once you have it.

To get the most from this book, it's vital that you begin putting the Diamond Rule into action **today.** That's why I've placed an **Exercises for Action** section at the end of each chapter. In the Exercises for Action, you will apply the information you learned to your world, so you can more fully create the life you desire and deserve. Please complete these exercises in a journal or notebook.

So let's get started on our journey to mastering the art of Giving People What They Really Want. Turn to Section 1 now to learn more about the Diamond Rule.

1

The Diamond Rule

In the Introduction, you learned that the Diamond Rule is, "Treat others in the unique way they want to be treated." This definition raises two questions:

1. What is it that people really want in life?

2. How can I discover what they really want in life?

That's exactly what you'll learn in this Section. In Chapter 1, "The 'What' and 'How' of Relationships," you'll learn the answer to question #1 above. In Chapter 2, "Values Are the 'What,'" and Chapter 3, "Sparks Are the 'How,'" you'll learn the answer to question #2 above.

CHAPTER

1

The "What" and "How" of Relationships

Let's play a quick game. On a sheet of paper, write anything you want in your life. Now, circle all your answers that are *emotions*, such as love, security, or freedom. The answers you didn't circle are probably things or experiences, such as money, a car, a home, a job, or a specific relationship. Next, complete this statement about all the items you didn't circle above: "If I had (the item you didn't circle—money, a job, etc.), it would give me (an emotion—freedom, security, happiness, etc.)." For example, "If I had a home it would give me happiness," or "If I had a million dollars, it would give me security," or "If I had a relation-ship, it would give me love."

It always comes down to feelings in the end. People don't want money. They want the feelings they *think* the money will give them. Winning a million dollars in the lottery has actually screwed up some people's lives. The money not only didn't give them the positive feelings they thought it would, it gave them pain in the long term!

Question: What are the two best days of boat ownership? Many former boat owners would answer, "The day I bought it, and the day I sold it!" People don't want boats. They buy a boat *thinking* it will give them excitement or freedom. Afterwards, they discover owning a boat doesn't lead to the feelings they desired, and it's a pain in the rear to maintain. Then, they sell it as soon as possible.

What's the difference between a house and a home? It's the feelings of love and happiness that become connected to a particular residence. The best real estate professionals know this, and they make a lot of money selling homes, not houses.

People don't want cars. They want the emotions they believe a particular car will give them. Pontiac isn't selling cars. They're selling excitement! Mercedes and BMW aren't selling cars. They're selling status and prestige. Volvo isn't selling cars. They're selling safety and intelligence. Volvos get people who desperately want to be intelligent, such as people who have advanced college degrees or teachers, to link Volvo automobiles to the intelligence they desire!

Unfortunately, cigarette manufacturers know that, when it comes right down to it, people really want emotions. Take a close look at their advertisements sometime. They never sell their product. They know that, in reality, their product has four main attributes: it's highly addictive, it's expensive, it stinks, and it kills people! Trying to push those four product features would be a tough sell in almost any market.

So, cigarette manufacturers don't sell cigarettes. They sell the emotions people want in their lives, and they very effectively link one or more of these feelings to their brand of cigarette. Marlboro has done the most effective job of doing this and, as a result, is the most popular brand in the United States. What emotions do the makers of Marlboro say you will receive from using their product? Think about the scenes in their ads before you answer. A typical ad has a ruggedly handsome cowboy comfortably sitting by a campfire smoking a cigarette. It's only he, his horse, the beautiful natural surroundings, and his cigarette. The only other image in the picture is a big pack of Marlboros down in the corner. The emotions Marlboro wants you to connect to their product are freedom, virility, individualism, and contentment—four emotions highly valued by many people in our society.

Think about it for a second. How much *logical* sense does it make to believe that becoming addicted to cigarettes will give you more freedom? Zero, zippo, none! But people don't do things for logical reasons. They do things for *emotional* reasons and sometimes justify their actions with logic. If people did things for logical reasons, men would be the ones riding sidesaddle! **People do things for emotional reasons. People want emotions.**

---◆---

People do things for emotional reasons.

---◆---

Let's take a more positive, yet equally effective, example from the world of advertising. In the decade prior to 1987, people in the U.S. were eating fewer and fewer raisins. It was really becoming a problem for the California Raisin Growers. Can you remember their advertising campaign before 1987? Most people can't because it was purely logical. It didn't have much impact. Remember the Sun•Maid Lady holding her parasol saying, "There's a drop of sunshine in every raisin. Eat raisins. They're good for you. They're healthy. They'll clean out your colon"?

Then in 1987, the Raisin Growers changed their advertising campaign to the Dancing Raisins. Their sales increased dramatically because they stopped trying to sell health and started selling fun! When I present programs to groups, I ask the audience, "How many of you liked watching the Dancing Raisins commercial?" Almost everyone in the room raises their hands. Then I ask them, "What song did they play in the background of the commercial?" Almost everyone answers, "Marvin Gaye's *I Heard It through the Grapevine.*"

Why do those commercials work so well? People watch the Dancing Raisins and feel good. Then one day or one week later they watch the commercial again. They see and hear the Dancing Raisins again and feel good again. After a few repetitions, the good feeling gets connected to the raisins in the nervous systems of the viewers! They become conditioned to want to eat raisins so they can feel good. They buy and eat raisins to get a positive feeling. The commercials are effective and memorable because they are *emotional!*

So now you've learned the first step to creating close relationships that prosper and last: *When it comes right down to it, people want emotions. When you consistently help people experience the unique emotions they desire, you're living by the Diamond Rule.*

In my opinion, the old saying that "knowledge is power" is missing a key ingredient. I believe that "knowledge immediately put into action is power!" Take action now by completing the following Exercises for Action and writing your answers in your journal or notebook. The power and joy of enhanced relationships await you.

EXERCISES FOR ACTION

1. Now that you've read Chapter 1, try again to think of anything you want in life that doesn't eventually boil down to an emotion. If you come up with an answer that isn't an emotion, repeatedly ask yourself, "If I had that, what *feeling* would it give me?" I believe you'll see that it always comes down to emotions.

2. Ask a few of your family members, friends, and/or associates at work, "If you could have anything in the world, what would it be?" If the answer isn't an emotion, keep asking, "If you had that, what *feeling* would it give you?" Again, I believe you'll notice that what people really want are emotions.

3. For one week, analyze all the television and print ads you see. What emotions are the advertisers trying to connect to their products?

In this chapter, you've learned the first key to giving people what they really want. **Key #1 is: When it comes right down to it, people want positive emotions in their lives.** In the next chapter, you'll learn that "not all emotions are created equal."

Read on to discover why . . . **Values Are the "What."**

2

Values
Are the "What"

O
n the next page are five emotions you may desire in your life. I could have listed hundreds of emotions, but I kept the list short to simplify the exercise. From this list of five emotions, pick the one that is **most important** to you in your life—the one feeling you desire most. If you have difficulty deciding between two emotions, ask yourself this question: "If I could only have one of these two emotions, which would I choose?" Write this emotion in your journal or notebook.

LOVE

SECURITY

ADVENTURE

SUCCESS

FREEDOM

From the four remaining emotions, select the one that is *next* most important to you. Do this two more times until you have put the five emotions in order, from most important to least important. Write all your answers in your journal or notebook.

The emotion you selected first is the one you value more than the others. It's the emotion that's most important for you to experience in your life. This emotion is your highest **Value** in life.

As you might imagine, not everyone would order the emotions the way you did. **People value emotions differently.** This variety is what makes the world an interesting and challenging place in which to live. To practice the Diamond Rule—which means giving people what they really want in all the relationships of your life—you must understand *their* unique set of Values.

----------◆----------

Values are the feelings people most want to experience.

----------◆----------

Let me share a personal example of Values in action. At one time in my life, I was a very successful dentist. I had a huge dental practice and was making tons of money. But I absolutely hated being tied down to the "drilling, filling, and billing" of dentistry. So I sold my practice and got completely out of the profession. Today, as a speaker and author, I choose the projects I want to work on and travel the world sharing ideas I believe in. Our house is on the top of a hill. We can see 25 miles into the distance from our back yard. For recreation, I frequently go scuba diving or do some other outdoor activity such as skiing, tennis, or golf.

From this small slice of my life I'll bet you can figure out which of the five emotions I value most in life. *Freedom* is at the top of my list. When I have freedom, I have the space to love others, be successful, and have adventure in my life. I'm attracted to jobs that give me freedom, sports that provide freedom, and other people who value freedom. My wife, Dawn, also puts freedom at the top of her list. Many times during the year I'll leave town for more than a week. Does Dawn cuddle up to me as I'm walking out the door and whisper gently in my ear, "I really wish you didn't have to go"? Heck no! She says, "See ya! Don't call home 'cause I probably won't be here!" Our relationship works well because we have a #1 Life Value in common. It is true that we have had some "interesting" discussions on what freedom is, but that's the subject of the next chapter.

If you're thinking right now that some other emotion ought to be #1, that just means you have a different set of Values concerning what a "good" marriage should be. We all have a tendency to believe that "my Values are the right Values!"

What emotion of the five do you think would be lowest on my list? If you guessed security, you're absolutely correct. Security doesn't appeal to me at all. When things get too secure in my life, I consciously and unconsciously shake them up!

Here's an example of the potential danger of not knowing someone's Values. Occasionally, I'll talk to a financial planner who is trying to sell me an investment plan. What emotion do you think he tries to sell me nine times out of ten? Security! It's truly amazing and amusing to see the sales process unfold. In the beginning of the sales call, the planner will ask me, "At what age do you want to retire?" I answer, "Retire from what? I never want to retire. I'm having way too much fun to retire!"

You should see the look on his face. He doesn't know what to do! It completely screws up his sales presentation because he can't pull out his handy-dandy little chart that shows how much money I need put away each year to comfortably retire at age 65. Then he will say something that sounds to me like, "Well, don't you want to build a nest egg so you can retire in Yuma, Arizona to an old person depository and play shuffleboard every afternoon and bingo on Wednesday evenings?" That vision of the future makes me sick. I want to keep "working" until I drop, and eventually have a fantastic place in the mountains where my family and I can ski, hike, bike, and enjoy all the freedom the world has to offer. If a financial planner would sell me a plan that would give me freedom, I'd be all ears.

When I do the **LOVE, SECURITY, ADVENTURE, SUCCESS, FREEDOM** exercise with a room full of people, each emotion is selected as #1 by at least 10% of the room. When I'm in a room full of salespeople, success and freedom are selected most often. When I'm in a room full of social workers, love is the #1 choice. This is another indication that people have different Values, and tend to choose careers that give them their highest Values.

I had an interesting and enlightening experience when doing this exercise in Malaysia in 1994. Most of the people in the room couldn't choose a highest Value from my usual list of **LOVE, SECURITY, ADVENTURE, SUCCESS,** and **FREEDOM.** I could see from their facial expressions they were in real pain trying to make a decision. Finally, they told me, "We don't want most of the emotions on your list!" With their input, I changed the list to:

CHARM

GRACE

LOVE

TRANSCENDENCE

PEACE

Different cultures often have different Values. To truly understand a culture, you must understand their Values! Likewise, to truly understand a person and give them what they really want, you must know their unique set of Values.

Let's review what you've learned so far:

1. When it comes right down to it, people want emotions.

2. Values are the emotions people want most.

3. Each person has a unique set of Values.

4. In order to give the person what he/she really wants, you must discover his/her Values.

DISCOVERING A PERSON'S VALUES

To discover a person's Values, follow this simple, yet profound, advice: "Ask and you shall receive." You will be amazed at what people will tell if you have a moderate level of rapport with them, and if they feel you have their best interests at heart. To be an effective Values detective, follow these five steps:

1. If you don't have it already, gain some rapport with the person. Be friendly and caring. If you have just met the person, engage in small talk to break the ice, and/or ask the person about things that interest him/her.

2. Let the person know **why** you're asking these questions. If you want to explore a co-worker's Values, say something like, "Mary, I really want to know the people I work with because everyone is different and everyone has different wants and needs. Tell me ..." (then go to the Values Question given in Step 3).

3.
Ask the Values Question: **"What's most important to you in (the Values area you want to explore)?"** The exact question you ask will be determined by your relationship with the person and the Values area you want to explore. For example, if you want to discover someone's Life Values, you would ask, "What's most important to you in life?" If you're a mother and you want to discover your son's Values in his relationship with you, you would ask, "What's most important to you in a relationship with a mom?" If you have a key associate at work, it would be valuable to ask the question, "What's most important to you in a relationship with an associate?" In Chapters 4 through 9, you will learn the precise Values Questions you need to ask in the most important relationships of your life.

4.
If you want to discover a second Value for a particular Values area, ask, **"What *else* is important to you in (the Values area you want to explore)?"** For example, "What else is important to you in a relationship with an associate?" The number of Values you discover depends on the depth of your relationship and the amount of time you have with the person.

5.
If you elicit more than one Value, make sure you put them in order by asking, "If you could have only one of these emotions, which one would you choose?" And then ask this question of each of the remaining Values until the entire list is in order from most important (#1) to least important.

Now it's time to apply the information in this chapter to your life by completing the Exercises for Action on the next page. Please do them now before you read on.

EXERCISES FOR ACTION

1. Think of a poor relationship you've had in the past*. As you might expect, the person probably had a different set of Values than you. In your journal or notebook, record what you think the difference was.

2. If you currently have a relationship with a person from a different culture, how do the Values of his/her culture differ from your culture's Values? Record your answer in your journal or notebook.

The subject of this chapter has been Values. Values are **what** people really want in their lives. The subject of the next chapter is Sparks. **Sparks are the things that *have to happen* for people to experience their Values.** Sparks are **how** they want it.

Intrigued? Read on to discover why... **Sparks Are the "How."**

*You will examine your current relationships in Chapters 4 through 9. In these six chapters, you will actually discover people's Values with the Values Question. The two exercises on this page are designed to stimulate your thinking about Values.

3

Sparks Are the "How"

Have you ever played a game with someone who had a different set of rules? What happened when you played the game for a period of time? There was some conflict, right? Both of you were upset because the other person didn't know the "rules of the game" (i.e., your rules!). To keep the game going, you had to reach an agreement on the rules in question.

The same thing happens in real life. Say you're in an important relationship with a person. Even if you have a common set of Values, each of you has a set of rules concerning the relationship and how it "should" work. Because people are different, the two sets of rules are probably different. Unless you get clear on the rules, there will probably be conflict.

In this book, the word we will use for rules is *Sparks*. **Sparks are the things that have to happen for people to experience their Values.** Like a spark is necessary to start a fire, or a spark plug is necessary to make your car run, a Spark is something that must happen for someone to "light the fire" of their Value.

Each person's Sparks for their Values are unique. And just like a game of football, this unique set of rules determines how they want to play the relationship "game" with you.

———————◆———————

Sparks are the things that have to happen for people to experience their Values.

———————◆———————

But giving people what they really want in life is more than just avoiding conflict. It's proactively discovering *what* people want (their Values) and *how* they want it (their Sparks). Now you can give them what they want in the way they want it on a consistent basis.

Here's an example of Values and Sparks in action. Love is a Value that is high on most people's Values lists. It is for my wife, Dawn, and me. If you've ever been in love, you know that different people have different Sparks for what has to happen for them to feel love. In our relationship, I could never *tell* Dawn I love her and it wouldn't bother her one bit! It's not one of her Sparks for love. She feels love when we go places and do things together—when we share experiences. If you're shaking your head in amazement, it just means that you have different Sparks for love than Dawn. If you're nodding in approval right now, it means that you have the same Spark for love as Dawn. I want my wife to feel loved. So, what do I do on a regular basis? I plan trips where we go places and do things together.

Speaking of the different Sparks people have for love, I once did a program for a large audience. I had them do the **LOVE, SECURITY, ADVENTURE, SUCCESS, FREEDOM** exercise you did in Chapter 2. As I read the five Values one at a time, I had the people in the audience raise their hands if they had that Value as their #1 choice. There were two women sitting next to each other who both raised their hands when I said "Love."

The woman on the left had a lot of pain in her body. There were deep frown lines in her face that had obviously been there a while, and her posture was extremely tight. I immediately knew there was a very good chance she wasn't getting much love in her life. To confirm my suspicion, I asked her the question, "What has to happen for you to experience love in your life?" She paused, then answered, "I'll be loved when I'm married to this one man." I asked, "Who's the guy?" She answered, "My ex-husband." Talk about opening a can of worms! I found out later that she had had a very messy divorce six months earlier. She was still attached to the guy, but he had moved on.

The woman's highest Value was love. Her Spark for love was being married to an ex-husband who wanted nothing to do with her. This woman had set up her life so she couldn't win. It's sad, isn't it—and have you ever done a similar thing in your life? Incidentally, I talked to the woman in private after the program and showed her how her Spark for love was leading to unhappiness, and suggested some other Sparks that would help her feel love on a daily basis.

The second woman also raised her hand when I said "Love." As I looked at her, I saw that she had a high degree of love and positive energy radiating from her body. I immediately knew she was getting a lot of love in her life. To confirm my assumption, I asked her the same question as the first woman: "What has to happen for you to experience love in your life?" She said, "I feel love whenever anyone smiles at me, does anything for me, or talks to me in a kind way. I feel love when I'm with my family, friends, or people here at work. I feel love whenever I smile at people, talk to them, or help them in any way." You could hear the whole room saying, "Ohhh!" The contrast between the two women's rules for the Love Game was striking.

The second woman's Spark for experiencing love was so all-inclusive that she felt the emotion frequently. She set up her game of life so she could win on a regular basis. Both of these women had the same #1 Value—love. However, they had two vastly different sets of Sparks for what had to happen for them to experience love. The first woman's Spark led to an absence of love. The second woman's Sparks led to an abundance of love.

The purpose of this book is not to help you examine your personal Values and Sparks (although I hope I've stimulated your thinking on the subject). The purpose of this book is to help you understand the principle of Values and Sparks, the power of the Diamond Rule, and how to discover other people's Values and Sparks in the key relationships of your life.

Here's a different example of the power of understanding other people's Values and Sparks. About five years ago I did a sales training program for a group of 300 people from a wide variety of organizations. After the program was over, a man came up to me and said, "I need some help. I own a limousine service that's about to go broke. I've cut my prices as far as I can, and people still don't use my services. They call me on the phone and the first question they ask is, 'How much?' I tell them my fee schedule. Then I say, 'We have some excellent limousines staffed by courteous drivers.' About one out of ten calls me back."

I said, "I know why you're having so much trouble. You're not discovering people's Values and Sparks. There is no way that you can make the sale and then give them the service they desire unless you find out what people want and how they want it." I gave him two specific questions he needed to start asking in order to save his business. He was in pain, so I knew he would follow through.

He called me one month later and said, "Nate, I can hardly believe it! I'm selling eight out of ten people who call me now, and I've raised my prices 15%!" I said, "I'm not surprised. You're asking those questions I gave you, aren't you?" He said, "I sure am!" I said, "You're finally discovering what people really want and how they want it, aren't you?" He said, "You bet!"

He then told me the following story that illustrated the power of his newfound skill. "Two Mondays ago a woman called me and said she wanted a limo for Friday evening. Her first question was, 'How much?' I told her, 'We have several different plans depending on what you want from the evening. But first, would you mind answering a couple of questions? I really want to get to know the people I serve because everyone has different wants and needs.' She said, 'Sure.'

"Then I asked her the first question you taught me: '*What's most important to you* in your limousine ride on Friday evening?' She answered, 'Well, five of my lady friends and I are going out on the town, and we want a wild, crazy, outrageous evening!' I wrote down *wild, crazy, outrageous evening* on a piece of paper as her #1 Value for the limo ride.

"Then I asked her the second question you taught me. I said, 'That's great! Now, *what has to happen* in order for you to have that wild, crazy, outrageous evening?' She answered, 'You know what? We want a moon roof in the limo so all six of us can stick our heads through the roof and yell at the guys on the sidewalk.' On my sheet of paper, I wrote down *Spark #1—moon roof.*

"Then I asked her another question: *'What else has to happen* for you to have a wild, crazy, outrageous evening this Friday?' She answered, 'Well, we want to have some champagne in the limo.' I remembered what you told me, Nate, about how I had to be specific with a person's Sparks, so I asked her what kind of champagne she wanted. She said, 'Korbel Champagne.' I asked, 'Do you want Green Label or White Label Korbel?' She answered, 'The Green Label.' Then I asked, 'How many bottles do you want?' She said, 'Three bottles.' I wrote down on my piece of paper *Spark #2—Three bottles of Green Label Korbel Champagne.*

"Things were going so well I decided to go for her third Spark. I asked her, *'What else would we have to do* for you to have a wild, crazy, outrageous evening this Friday?' She enthusiastically answered, 'We want to have a guy driver. We want him to be young and outgoing. We want someone we can really talk to and who will talk to us. Ya know what? We want a stud!' I wrote down *Spark #3— Stud driver.*"

Do you see what's happening here? My friend is learning exactly what the woman wants and how she wants it. He's being precise in his discovery of her Values and Sparks. Remember what he used to say to all his prospects? "We have some excellent limos staffed by courteous drivers." She doesn't want an excellent limo staffed by a courteous driver. She wants a stud who's driving a moon-roofed limo loaded with three bottles of chilled Green Label Korbel Champagne!

Armed with this information, how difficult was it for him to make the sale? Extremely easy! He told her, "This Friday you and your guests will have our finest limousine, Silver Cloud #7. It has a double moon roof so up to eight people can stand up and yell at the guys on the sidewalk. I'll have three bottles of chilled Green Label Korbel Champagne waiting for you, and do you know who your driver will be? Crazy Larry. He's young, outgoing—a real stud. You'll have a wild, crazy, outrageous time with him!"

My friend quoted her a price that was 15% higher than the competition. Do you think he got the job? Sure. Why? Because he showed her how she could get exactly what she wanted in the way she wanted it with his limousine service. Then on Friday night, he gave her the service he promised. After he did that, do you think she will use his service again? Absolutely. Do you think she will refer her friends to him? Positively.

I hope you see the power in discovering people's Values and Sparks in all the relationships of your life. In the last chapter you learned the Values Questions to discover *what* people want. Now it's time to learn the Sparks Questions to discover *how* they want it.

DISCOVERING A PERSON'S SPARKS

1. After you learn the person's first Value with the Values Question, discover one or more of their Sparks for that Value only. After you have done that, you can discover Value #2 and the Sparks for that Value.

2. Ask the Sparks Question, **"What has to happen in order for you to feel (the Value you just learned)?"** In the limousine example, the Sparks Question was, "What has to happen for you to have a wild, crazy, outrageous evening this Friday?" The first Spark discovered was, "A moon roof."

3. There may be multiple Sparks for each Value. To discover these additional Sparks, ask the question, **"What else has to happen in order for you to feel (the Value you just learned)?"** The Sparks Question can be worded differently depending on the situation. In the limousine example, the second Sparks Question was, "What else has to happen for you to have a wild, crazy, outrageous evening this Friday?" Her second Spark discovered was, "Three bottles of Green Label Korbel Champagne." Her third Spark was, "A stud driver."

--- ◆ ---

"What has to happen in order for you to feel (the Value you just learned)?"

--- ◆ ---

As you will see in Chapters 4 through 9, there are many ways to word the Values and Sparks Questions. The exact wording isn't as important as making the Diamond Rule a guiding principle in all the relationships in your world. Living a life based on discovering what people want, how they want it, and then giving it to them when it's in their best long-term interest will also bring *you* the emotions you desire and deserve.

Have you ever had a relationship with someone that ended on a sour note, and you didn't know what happened? You now have the tools to revisit that relationship to discover exactly why it ended. That's what you will do in this chapter's Exercises for Action. Do them now while the information is fresh in your mind.

EXERCISES FOR ACTION

1. Think of a **business** relationship you've had that was basically good, but it went through a difficult period of time or ended because you broke one of the other person's rules. What was the rule you broke? What upset did that create? How did you resolve the upset (i.e., did you get clear on the rules of the game)? Record your answers in your journal or notebook.

2. Think of a **personal** relationship you've had that was basically a good one, but went through a difficult period of time or ended because you broke one of the other person's rules. What was the rule you broke? What upset did that create? How did you resolve the upset (i.e., did you get clear on the rules of the game)? Record your answers in your journal or notebook.

Now that you know the power of discovering people's Values and Sparks, it's time to start applying your knowledge to the relationships in your life. Move on to Section Two and begin . . . **Applying the Diamond Touch.**

2

Applying the Diamond Touch

Let's review what you've learned so far.

1. When it comes right down to it, people want emotions.

2. **Values** are the emotions people want most.

3. Each person has a unique set of Values.

4. In order to give the person what he/she really wants, you must discover his/her Values.

5. **Sparks** are what has to happen for people to experience their Values. Each person has a unique set of Sparks for each of his/her Values.

6. In order to give the person what he/she really wants, you must discover his/her Values and the Sparks for each Value you discovered in #4 above.

In this Section, you will learn the exact questions you need to ask to discover the Values and Sparks for the people in six of the most important relationship categories in your life:

Chapter 4 Husband/Wife Relationships

Chapter 5 Parent/Child Relationships

Chapter 6 Friendships

Chapter 7 Work Relationships

Chapter 8 Influence Relationships

Chapter 9 Service Relationships

Read on. Your spouse, children, friends, associates at work, prospects, customers and clients are waiting!

4

Husband/Wife Relationships

I've purposely put the Husband/Wife Relationships chapter first in this Section because these are the most important relationships in many people's lives. In my opinion, more marriages and other intimate relationships have ended because:

1. One or both people in the relationship didn't accurately *discover* the other person's Values and Sparks, and then

2. One or both people in the relationship didn't consistently *give* the other person what they

wanted in the way they wanted it (when it was in the other person's best long-term interest).

I know this may sound overly simplistic, but from my personal relationship track record and from observing other people's relationship histories, I believe it's true. Take a second now to check it out in your own life. Think of an important relationship in your life that ended with an upset. What Value(s) and Spark(s) of *yours* were broken? What Value(s) and Spark(s) of the *other person* were broken? Record your answers in your journal or notebook.

Now answer a vitally important question. How might things have been different if both of you had accurately **discovered** the other person's Values and Sparks, and then **given** the other person what he/she wanted in the way he/she wanted it (when it was in his/her best long-term interest)? Record your answers in your journal or notebook.

A profound yet simple principle, isn't it? But in it there is tremendous and easily accessible power **when** you apply it effectively in your relationships!

———————◆———————

The trouble with man is twofold.
He cannot learn truths which are too complicated:
and he forgets truths which are too simple.

REBECCA WEST

———————◆———————

I hope I have your attention! I also hope that you will use the following Values and Sparks Discovery Process with your husband, wife, or significant other.

THE VALUES AND SPARKS DISCOVERY PROCESS FOR A MARRIAGE

*First, explain to your spouse **why** you want to ask these questions. Of course, the best way to do this is to study this book together.*

A. Explore the Relationship Values Area.

1. Ask the Values Question, "What's most important to you in a relationship with a husband/wife?" Discover his/her #1 Value for this area.

2. For the Value you discovered in Step 1 above, ask the Sparks Question, "What has to happen in order for you to feel (#1 Value)?" Discover his/her first Spark for the #1 Value.

3. Discover at least two other Sparks for his/her #1 Value by asking, "What else has to happen in order for you to feel (#1 Value)?"

4. Discover at least two other Values for the Relationship Values area by asking, "What else is important to you in a relationship with a husband/wife?" Then repeat Steps 2 and 3 to discover at least two Sparks for each additional Value you discover.

B. Explore the Life Values Area.

1. Ask the Values Question, "What's most important to you in life?" Discover his/her #1 Value for this area.

2. For the Value you discovered in Step 1 above, ask the Sparks Question, "What has to happen in order for you to feel (#1 Value)?" Discover his/her first Spark for the #1 Value.

3. Discover at least two other Sparks for his/her #1 Value by asking, "What else has to happen in order for you to feel (#1 Value)?"

4. Discover at least two other Values for the Life Values area by asking, "What else is important to you in life?" Then repeat Steps 2 and 3 to discover at least two Sparks for each additional Value you discover.

When you use the Values and Sparks Discovery Process with your spouse, be prepared to learn more about him/her in one hour than you have over the course of your entire relationship. Be prepared to gain the information you will need to make a dramatic, consistent, and long-lasting improvement in the quality of the relationship!

---◆---

A Value is always an *emotion*. A Spark is *something that has to happen* for the person to feel the emotion.

---◆---

ADDITIONAL INSIGHTS

1. If the person gives you a Spark when you ask the Values Question, just say, "That's great! If you had (the Spark they gave you), what would that mean to you? What would that give you?" Remember, a Value is always an *emotion*. A Spark is *something that has to happen* for the person to feel the emotion.

2. If the person is giving you a series of Sparks when you're asking the Values Question, you may have to mentally analyze the Sparks and suggest a Value. Say, "It sounds like (the Value you believe the person is referring to) is very important to you." For example, if someone says, "You have to listen to me and not contradict me in front of other people," your response might be, "It sounds like respect is important to you. Is that right?" The person will verbally and nonverbally tell you if you guessed right. If you're wrong, guess again.

3. If you ask a question, and the person says, "I don't know," don't let him/her off the hook. He/she does know. The person probably just hasn't thought about it in a while. Just come back with, "I know you don't know, but if you did know, what would the answer be?" Or, "I know it may be hard to think right now, but just give me something off the top of your head." Be politely persistent.

4. If the person has trouble coming up with a Spark for a specific Value, have him/her remember a specific time when he/she deeply felt the Value. What was happening in the moment that sparked him/her to feel the emotion? For example, if the Value you discovered for your spouse was love, and he/she is having trouble coming up with a Spark, ask, "Can you remember a time when you felt deeply loved? What was happening that sparked the feeling of love?"

5. Be sure that each Spark is worded in a *positive* way. If the person words the Spark in a negative way, clarify what the positive would be. As an example, if your spouse says, "I feel loved when you don't ignore me at parties," you can respond, "Good! What can I do at parties to show you I love you and enjoy myself?"

6. Be certain that the person is very *specific* on his/her Sparks. Remember my friend with the limousine company. It was much better for him to discover the

woman wanted "three bottles of Green Label Korbel Champagne" rather than "some champagne." The Spark should be specific enough that you know exactly what you can do to give the person what he/she wants.

7. Occasionally, you may want to word a Sparks Question in a way that focuses the person's attention on what **you** can do to give them their Values. For example, if the person says he/she wants love in his/her life, you can ask, "What do I do now, or what could I do in the future, that would make you feel the most love?"

8. The number of Values and Sparks you discover depends on the depth of your relationship and the amount of time you have spent with the person. Lots of depth and time (i.e., in most intimate relationships) equals many Values and Sparks. Little depth and time (i.e., with an occasional customer at your business) equals few Values and Sparks.

9. You can word the Values and Sparks Questions differently depending on the situation and the kinds of answers the person is giving you. You can see this in the examples I've used in this and subsequent chapters. The Values and Sparks Discovery Process is much more than a series of specific questions. It's a consistent way of thinking that can be summed up as, "What do they want (their Values), and how do they want it (their Sparks)?"

10. Get permission to write down people's answers. This will make the process even more important to them.

11. As you go through the Values and Sparks Discovery Process, do not be judgmental! This will guarantee an abrupt end to the process. Just because you discover a person's Values and Sparks does not mean that you *agree* with them, or that you are planning on giving the person exactly what he/she wants. Depending on the nature of the relationship, you may have to negotiate "the rules of the game" or, in relationships where education of one of the players is important (e.g., parent/child), you may have to educate them. In Chapter 16, you will learn how to do this, as well as what to do if you believe the Values and/or Sparks are not in the person's best long-term interest.

12. If the person is resistant to the Values and Sparks Process, you need to gain more of their trust. Be sure he/she understands why you want the information, and/or proceed again at a more convenient time.

13. People's Values and Sparks change over time. Be sure to check in with the people in your close relationships at regular intervals.

14. In certain situations, it may be best to do the Values and Sparks Discovery Process with some lightness and humor. Make the process enjoyable, not like police are interrogating a suspect in an old "cops and robbers" movie.

15.

Be certain you come from a place of giving. You're learning this information so that you can do a better job of giving people what they want in the way they want it. You are also giving people the gift of self-understanding. This may be the first time they have consciously examined their Values and Sparks in a relationship— which is valuable in and of itself. After you discover their Values and Sparks, they may volunteer to reverse roles, or it may be appropriate for you to ask them to elicit your Values and Sparks as well.

An Example of the Husband/Wife Values Discovery Process

Wife   "Honey, I really want to make our relationship even better than it already is. To do that, I need to learn more precisely what you want in our relationship and in life. After I'm done, you can ask me the same questions if you'd like."

Husband   "Sounds like you've been watching Oprah again."

Wife   "Actually, I've been reading this book. Do you want to take a look?"

Husband	"That's okay. Ask away."
Wife	"I like to start with the easy questions. When it comes right down to it, what's most important to you in a relationship with a wife?" (The Values Question to discover his #1 Relationship Value)
Husband	"Oh, I don't know. A lot of things." (Typical unspecific "guy" answer)
Wife	"Of all those things on the list, which would be most important?" (A question that elegantly guides him to be specific)
Husband	"Well, I guess being respected." (His #1 Relationship Value)
Wife	"Great! What do I do right now, or what could I do, to make you feel respected?" (A form of the Sparks Question)
Husband	"I don't know."
Wife	"I know it's kind of hard to think of something right now, but just give me something off the top of your head." (She's wisely not taking "I don't know" for an answer.)
Husband	"Boy, I really can't think of anything."
Wife	"Can you remember a time when you really felt respected by me?" (She directs his focus to the past.)

Husband   "Well, yeah."

Wife   "When was that, and what did I do that gave you the feeling?"

Husband   "It was the time when I got my first promotion at work. You hugged me and told me how proud you were of me!" (She finally gets his #1 Spark for the Value of respect. Now, she has one way to show him respect. She can obtain more by asking the following question.)

Wife   "That's great, honey. What else has to happen for you to feel respect? What's another way you feel truly respected? " (A Sparks Question for the respect Value)

Husband   "You're persistent, aren't you? Well, I feel respected when you don't criticize me." (Have you ever had a conversation in your marriage that started like this? Now is the time to get some resolution on how you can communicate your desires while your spouse maintains his/her respect.)

Wife   "What can I do when I don't like something you've done, so I can get my point across *and* you can feel respected?" (She's turning his negative "Don't criticize me" into a positive "What can I do," *and* discovering a way where both of their desires can be met.)

Husband   "You can say you don't like what I just did without making me seem like I was wrong. You can *ask* me not to do something instead of *demanding* that I don't do it."

Wife   "That sounds fair enough. Will you remind me if I fall back into my old routine?"

Husband   "Sure!" (He's liking the process better already!)

The wife would now discover more Sparks for the Value of respect. Then she would discover more Values and Sparks in the area of a husband/wife relationship. Now she can move on to the Life Values area.

Wife   "Here's another easy question. What's most important to you in life?"

Husband   "Doing well at work." (She asks a Values Question, but he answers with a Spark.)

Wife   "If you did well at work, what would that mean to you?"

Husband   "It would mean that I would be moving ahead." (He gives her another Spark.)

Wife   "If you were moving ahead, what would that mean to you?"

Husband	"It would mean that I might get a promotion." (He gives her a third Spark.)
Wife	"It sounds to me like being successful is very important to you?" (She doesn't want to continue chasing Sparks and suggests the Value of success.)
Husband	"You're right. Success is very important to me." (Hooray! She guessed correctly.)
Wife	"One of the things you mentioned that had to happen for you to have success was that you had to do well at work. Can you be more specific?"
Husband	"I do well at work when I feel good about the quality of my work." (His first Spark for success)
Wife	"What can I do to help you move ahead at work, feel good about your work, and be more successful?"
Husband	"Every once in a while, I need to bring work home. When I do, I need to go to my cave and be left alone for a couple of hours."
Wife	"The family and I can do that as long as it doesn't happen more than once a week. Is that fair?" (She's negotiating a Spark that will work for everyone involved.)
Husband	"Sure."
Wife	"What else has to happen for you to feel success in your life?" (She's after his second Spark for success.)

Husband "I feel successful when I'm recognized for my achievements." (His second Spark for success is being recognized.)

Wife "Specifically, how do you like to be recognized?" (She wants some clarity so she knows exactly what she can do.)

Husband "Awards are nice, but verbal congratulations are better."

Wife "What else has to happen for you to feel success in your life?" (She's on a roll now!)

Husband "I'll feel successful when we can put away $10,000 a year for retirement." (His third Spark for success in his life is putting $10,000 a year into a retirement account.)

The wife can now discover more Sparks for the Life Value of success. Then she can discover more Values and the Sparks that go with them in the Life Values area. As you may have noticed, she told him a couple of ways she can give him what he wants in life in the way he wants it. At the end of the conversation, she can look over her notes and see many other ways that she can be a caring Values and Sparks provider. See Chapter 16 for more ideas.

As you might imagine, the Exercises for Action section is especially comprehensive for this chapter, *and* it's extremely important that you complete it this week. You now have a nugget of knowledge. Turn that knowledge into power by doing the Exercises for Action with your spouse or significant other tonight.

EXERCISES FOR ACTION

THE VALUES AND SPARKS DISCOVERY PROCESS FOR A MARRIAGE

*First, explain to your partner **why** you want to ask these questions. Of course, the best way to do this is to study this book together. Record all of your answers in your journal or notebook.*

A. Explore the Relationship Values Area.

1. Ask the Values Question, "What's most important to you in a relationship with a husband/wife?" Discover his/her #1 Value for this area.

2. For the Value you discovered in Step 1 above, ask the Sparks Question, "What has to happen in order for you to feel (#1 Value)?" Discover his/her first Spark for the #1 Value.

3. Discover at least two other Sparks for his/her #1 Value by asking, "What else has to happen in order for you to feel (#1 Value)?"

4. Discover at least two other Values for the Relationship Values area by asking, "What else is important to you in a relationship with a husband/wife?" Then repeat Steps 2 and 3 to discover at least two Sparks for each additional Value you discover.

B. Explore the Life Values Area.

1. Ask the Values Question, "What's most important to you in life?" Discover his/her #1 Value for this area.

2. For the Value you discovered in Step 1 above, ask the Sparks Question, "What has to happen in order for you to feel (#1 Value)?" Discover his/her first Spark for the #1 Value.

3. Discover at least two other Sparks for his/her #1 Value by asking, "What else has to happen in order for you to feel (#1 Value)?"

4. Discover at least two other Values for the Life Values area by asking, "What else is important to you in life?" Then repeat Steps 2 and 3 to discover at least two Sparks for each additional Value you discover.

In this chapter, you learned the Values and Sparks Discovery Process for Husband/Wife relationships. In the next chapter, you will move on to another important relationship—the Parent/Child relationship.

Parent/Child relationships can be especially challenging for two reasons:

1. You have two unique people with different Values and Sparks.

2. The two people are from different generations. Generations have different sets of Values and Sparks that are reinforced by the members of that generation. This is usually referred to as the generation gap.

I know that you're up to the challenge. After you complete this chapter's Exercises for Action, read on to discover how you can improve your . . . **Parent/Child Relationships.**

5

Parent/Child Relationships

Here's a short example of the Values and Sparks Discovery Process used in a mother/son relationship. Anthony Robbins' wife, Becky, once asked her son, Josh, "What's most important to you in a relationship with a mom?" He answered, "Love." She then said, "That's great, Josh. I really want you to feel loved. What can I do to make you feel the most loved?" Josh answered, "Tickle my toes when you tuck me in bed at night."

Becky vaguely knew that Josh liked having his toes tickled, but she never knew it was **that** important. So what did she do on a regular basis to make him feel more loved? Tickled his toes when she tucked him in bed at night.

Having my toes tickled isn't **my** #1 Spark for love. But that's what makes life so interesting and challenging: we're all "wired" differently when it comes to the pleasure we desire and how we want that pleasure delivered. The Values and Sparks Discovery Process is the best method I know to learn the "wiring plan" of the people with whom we have relationships.

Sometimes it seems to adults that children are "wired" in an incomprehensible fashion. That's why it's especially important for you to do the following Values and Sparks Discovery Process with your children.

THE VALUES AND SPARKS DISCOVERY PROCESS FOR A PARENT/CHILD RELATIONSHIP

*First, explain to your child **why** you want to ask these questions. Let them know that you love them and want to get to know them better.*

A. Explore the Relationship Values Area.

1. Ask this Values Question: "What's most important to you in a relationship with a mom/dad?" Discover your child's #1 Value for this area.

2. For the Value you discovered in Step 1, ask the Sparks Question, "What has to happen in order for you to feel (#1 Value)?" Discover his/her first Spark for the #1 Value.

3. Discover at least two other Sparks for his/her #1 Value by asking, "What else has to happen in order for you to feel (#1 Value)?"

4. Discover three other Values for the Relationship Values area by asking, "What else is important to you in a relationship with a mom/dad?" Then repeat Steps 2 and 3 to discover at least two Sparks for each additional Value you discover.

B. Explore the Life Values Area.

1. Ask this Values Question: "What's most important to you in life?" Discover your child's #1 Value for this area.

2. For the Value you discovered in Step 1 above, ask the Sparks Question, "What has to happen in order for you to feel (#1 Value)?" Discover his/her first Spark for the #1 Value.

3. Discover at least two other Sparks for his/her #1 Value by asking, "What else has to happen in order for you to feel (#1 Value)?"

4. Discover at least two other Values for the Life Values area by asking, "What else is important to you in life?"

Then repeat Steps 2 and 3 to discover at least two Sparks for each additional Value you discover.

An Example of Using the Values Discovery Process in a Parent/Child Relationship

I have a wonderful teenage daughter, Belinda. About a year ago, I did the Values Discovery Process with her. Here's an edited version of how it went.

Nate "Belinda, I really want to be the best possible dad I can. In order for me to do that, I'd like to know what's really important to you. This is the same kind of thing we talked about a year ago. Is it okay if I ask you those questions again?"

Belinda "Sure, Dad."

Nate "What's most important to you in a relationship with a dad?" (The Values Question to discover her #1 Value)

Belinda "Oh, probably having fun." (Her #1 Value)

Nate "That's great! What kinds of things do I do now, or what things could I do with you or for you, so that you would have the most fun?" (A form of the Sparks Question)

Belinda "I like it when we go to the Family Fun Center together." (Her first Spark for Value #1. I thought that she didn't enjoy going there as much as she used to. I learned that was not the case.)

Nate   "What are a couple of other things that have to happen for us to have a lot of fun in our relationship?" (I'm after more Sparks for Value #1.)

Belinda   "I love when we go to the beach together, and when we travel as a family. I really like it when you and I go clothes shopping together for school." (Three more Sparks for Value #1)

Nate   "Is there something I can do almost every day that would be fun for us to do?" (I noticed that the Sparks she was giving me weren't things that I could do almost every day. I wanted to have fun with her on a regular basis.)

Belinda   "Hmmm, it's fun when we play our computer games together." (Her fifth Spark for Value #1, one that we can do regularly)

Nate   "In addition to having fun, what else is important to you in a relationship with a dad?" (Discovering relationship Value #2)

Belinda   "Caring is probably next important." (Her second Value in our relationship)

Nate   "That's neat. What can I do so you know I care about you?" (Discovering her first Spark for Value #2)

Belinda	"I feel that you care about me when you give me good advice." (This one blew my mind! A 12 year old wanting advice!)
Nate	"What's good advice to you, Belinda?" (I needed to get more clarity on what "good advice" was.)
Belinda	"Good advice is advice that helps me do better."

I went on to discover two more Sparks for Value #2. Then I discovered her third Value for our relationship, which was "love," and elicited four Sparks for that Value.

Next, I wanted to explore her **Life** Values area. I asked her these questions:

Nate	"Belinda, what's most important to you in life?"
Belinda	"Friends." (I asked the Values Question and she gave me a Spark. I wrote this down as Spark #1 under a yet-to-be-discovered Value.)
Nate	"If you had friends, what would that mean to you?" (I wanted to discover the Value that "having friends" would give her.)
Belinda	"If I had friends, then I would have self-esteem." (Self-esteem is an emotion, so it's her #1 Life Value. I then discovered more Sparks for the self-esteem Value.)

Nate	"In addition to self-esteem, what else is important to you in life?" (I wanted the second Life Value.)
Belinda	"A good education." (She gave me a Spark, so I asked a question that would elevate the Spark to a Value.)
Nate	"What would having a good education give you?"
Belinda	"Success." (Her second Life Value)

At this point we had a nice discussion on all the different ways that she could get a good education—college, reading, talking to people, educational TV, computers, etc. (Notice that the Discovery Process does more than reveal Values and Sparks. It is a valuable tool to help you pinpoint the areas where you need to educate your children.) I went on to discover a third Life Value.

Nate	"What else is important to you in life?"
Belinda	"To be popular." (I had a feeling we would have an interesting discussion here.)
Nate	"What has to happen for you to be popular?" (The Sparks Question)
Belinda	"When *everyone* likes me." (This is a Spark that is guaranteed to lead to lousy feelings. I knew it was time for some education. After all, Belinda said she wanted "good advice.")

Nate "Does *everyone* have to like you to be popular?'

Belinda "Well, I guess not. Just *some* of the kids would be okay."

Nate "How important is it to you that they like you for the right reasons? That they like you just because you're a great person?"

Belinda "Yeah, I guess you're right. Some kids do bad things to try to get liked."

Nate "So, if you happened to be with a bunch of kids who were taking drugs, and they put pressure on you to take drugs, you could say 'No' and get the heck out of there."

Belinda "Sure."

Nate "And if you did that, you would actually have more self-esteem, wouldn't you?" (Her #1 Life Value) "You would be more successful in life, wouldn't you?" (Her #2 Life Value) "*And* you would be still be popular with the right people for the right reasons, wouldn't you?" (Her #3 Life Value)

This is a great example of the power of knowing someone's Values. I could have preached to Belinda about the danger of drugs. Instead, I chose to link what she wanted most in her life to being drug free.

If you have kids and/or parents, it's time to put your knowledge into action by completing the Exercises for Action on the next page. It's best to do the Values Discovery Process in person, but if you have to use the phone, go for it. Just do it!

EXERCISES FOR ACTION

THE VALUES AND SPARKS DISCOVERY PROCESS FOR A PARENT/CHILD RELATIONSHIP

First, explain to your child **why** *you want to ask these questions. If your child is old enough, study this book together. You might want to review the Additional Insights on pages 37–41. Record all of your answers in your journal or notebook.*

A. Explore the Relationship Values Area.

1. Ask this Values Question: "What's most important to you in a relationship with a mom/dad?" Discover his/her #1 Value for this area.

2. For the Value you discovered in Step 1 above, ask the Sparks Question, "What has to happen in order for you to feel (#1 Value)?" Discover his/her first Spark for the #1 Value.

3. Discover at least two other Sparks for his/her #1 Value by asking, "What else has to happen in order for you to feel (#1 Value)?"

4. Discover three other Values for the Relationship Values area by asking, "What else is important to you in a relationship with a mom/dad?" Then repeat Steps 2 and 3 to discover at least two Sparks for each additional Value you discover.

B. Explore the Life Values Area.

1. Ask this Values Question: "What's most important to you in life?" Discover his/her #1 Value for this area.

2. For the Value you discovered in Step 1 above, ask the Sparks Question, "What has to happen in order for you to feel (#1 Value)?" Discover his/her first Spark for the #1 Value.

3. Discover at least two other Sparks for his/her #1 Value by asking, "What else has to happen in order for you to feel (#1 Value)?"

4. Discover at least two other Values for the Life Values area by asking, "What else is important to you in life?" Then repeat Steps 2 and 3 to discover at least two Sparks for each additional Value you discover.

Like the television program *Friends,* relationships with real-life friends can be challenging. After you've completed this chapter's Exercises for Action, read on to learn how you can improve your . . . **Friendships.**

6

Friendships

A friendship is an interesting and challenging form of relationship. Friendships come in all sorts of sizes, shapes, and colors. Some friendships are close. Some are more distant. Some friendships are new; others are old. In some friendships, you're with the person frequently. In others, you rarely see the person. Some friendships were initiated by you and the friend. Others involve a third person who is "the glue" in the relationship.

Some people have just one type of friend—someone who has similar Values and Sparks to theirs. This requires very little flexibility on the person's part in applying the Diamond Touch, because "we're just like two peas in a pod." Having only friends like this is certainly better than not having any friends at all, *and* it's been my experience that having a wide variety of friends expands your horizons. It opens up a whole new world of learning that you would never experience if you just hung around with the same old folks all the time. In order to have a wide variety of friends, however, you're going to want to be a master of the Diamond Touch.

Here are the questions to ask to discover your friend's Values and Sparks:

THE VALUES AND SPARKS DISCOVERY PROCESS FOR A FRIENDSHIP

*First, explain to your friend **why** you want to ask these questions. Of course, the best way to do this is to study this book together.*

A. Explore the Relationship Values Area.

1. Ask this Values Question: "What's most important to you in a relationship with a friend?" Discover his/her #1 Value for this area.

2. For the Value you discovered in Step 1 above, ask the Sparks Question, "What has to happen in order for you to feel (#1 Value)?" Discover his/her first Spark for the #1 Value.

3. Discover at least two other Sparks for his/her #1 Value by asking, "What else has to happen in order for you to feel (#1 Value)?"

4. Discover at least two other Values for the Relationship Values area by asking, "What else is important to you in a relationship with a friend?" Then repeat Steps 2 and 3 to discover at least two Sparks for each additional Value you discover.

B. Explore the Life Values Area.

1. Ask this Values Question: "What's most important to you in life?" Discover his/her #1 Value for this area.

2. For the Value you discovered in Step 1 above, ask the Sparks Question, "What has to happen in order for you to feel (#1 Value)?" Discover his/her first Spark for the #1 Value.

3. Discover at least two other Sparks for his/her #1 Value by asking, "What else has to happen in order for you to feel (#1 Value)?"

4. Discover at least two other Values for the Life Values area by asking, "What else is important to you in life?" Then repeat Steps 2 and 3 to discover at least two Sparks for each additional Value you discover.

One extremely important use of the Values and Sparks Discovery Process is to find out what went wrong after you've had an upset with someone. Whenever there's been an upset, it means that one or both of you have had your rules broken, i.e., a Spark for a high Value was being either ignored or stomped on! The following example of the Values and Sparks Discovery Process will illustrate just such a situation. Assume that your friend, Tanya, told you a story that she wanted you to keep confidential. You didn't realize this and told the story to another person. Tanya has just confronted you.

An Example of Using the Values and Sparks Process to Resolve an Upset in a Friendship

Tanya   "I've got a bone to pick with you. Why did you tell Maria what we talked about yesterday?" (She is telling you *how* a high Value of hers was broken.)

You   "Oh, I'm sorry. I didn't think you'd mind."

Tanya   "Of course I mind. It was personal. I didn't want anybody to know."

You   "It sounds like I broke your *trust* when I told Maria." (You suggest a Value that you believe was violated.)

Tanya   "You're darn right!" (Bingo.)

You   "I apologize. It wasn't my intent to hurt you. I didn't think you would mind if Maria knew. Let's make sure this doesn't happen again. How can you let me know if our conversation is confidential?" (You clarify the rules of the game. You identify what has to happen for information to be classified as confidential.)

Tanya   "I'll tell you if I want some information to be kept confidential." (She tells you what needs to be done differently so her Value of trust is not violated again.)

You   "Great. Now I know. In addition, is it okay for me to ask if I think something you tell me may be confidential?" (You add another safeguard to make sure the Value is not violated.)

Tanya   "Sure!" (Now, everyone knows the rules of the game.)

As you can see, it doesn't take long to heal upsets if you have the Diamond Touch.

When an upset occurs:

1.   Identify *how* the Value was violated.

2.   Identify *what* Value was violated.

3.   Identify what needs to be done differently so the violation doesn't happen again. You may need to negotiate this point to reach an agreement that's acceptable to both parties.

The next time you have an upset with someone, use the Diamond Touch and be amazed with the results.

I hope you've done at least one of the Exercises for Action sections in the last two chapters. If you have, the Values and Sparks Discovery Process should be coming more naturally to you. Let's continue the learning process by applying the method to your friendships.

EXERCISES FOR ACTION

THE VALUES AND SPARKS DISCOVERY PROCESS FOR A FRIENDSHIP

*First, explain to your friend **why** you want to ask these questions. Of course, the best way to do this is to study this book together. You might want to review the Additional Insights on pages 37–41. Record all of your answers in your journal or notebook.*

A. Explore the Relationship Values Area.

1. Ask this Values Question: "What's most important to you in a relationship with a friend?" Discover his/her #1 Value for this area.

2. For the Value you discovered in Step 1 above, ask the Sparks Question, "What has to happen in order for you to feel (#1 Value)?" Discover his/her first Spark for the #1 Value.

3. Discover at least two other Sparks for his/her #1 Value by asking, "What else has to happen in order for you to feel (#1 Value)?"

4. Discover at least two other Values for the Relationship Values area by asking, "What else is important to you in a relationship with a friend?" Then repeat Steps 2 and 3 to discover at least two Sparks for each additional Value you discover.

B. Explore the Life Values Area.

1. Ask this Values Question: "What's most important to you in life?" Discover his/her #1 Value for this area.

2. For the Value you discovered in Step 1 above, ask the Sparks Question, "What has to happen in order for you to feel (#1 Value)?" Discover his/her first Spark for the #1 Value.

3. Discover at least two other Sparks for his/her #1 Value by asking, "What else has to happen in order for you to feel (#1 Value)?"

4. Discover at least two other Values for the Life Values area by asking, "What else is important to you in life?" Then repeat Steps 2 and 3 to discover at least two Sparks for each additional Value you discover.

You spend approximately 2,000 hours a year at your place of work. Poor work relationships can make even the best job a pain in the neck. Positive work relationships can make going to the office a pleasure. Read on to learn how to use the Diamond Touch in your . . . **Work Relationships.**

CHAPTER **7**

Work Relationships

T

he average American corporation loses *half* its employees every four years. Here are some interesting statistics on why people leave one company for another. According to a 1996 survey conducted by the Customer Relations Institute of San Diego, the top three reasons for leaving a job were:

1. Frustrating management practices/ policies—52%

2. Limited opportunities for growth—13%

3. Low compensation—10%

The top two reasons for leaving a job (almost two-thirds of the total) are directly related to people not having their Values met. Money comes in a distant third!

Have you ever left a job for another one? Why did you leave? Was it strictly for money, or were there other factors involved? Write the answer in your notebook or journal.

Now analyze your answer by putting it through the Values and Sparks filter. When your Values are not being met and your Sparks are being broken, you feel pain. What Values were not being met and which Sparks were being broken on the job you left? Write your answer in your notebook or journal.

When you see an opportunity for your Values and Sparks to be met more completely with a new opportunity (i.e., a new job), you will want to take action to achieve it. In what ways did you see your Values and Sparks being met more completely with the new job? Write the answer in your notebook or journal.

Do you see how your Values and Sparks direct your behavior, and do you see why discovering your work associates' Values and Sparks is so important? When you are an expert at giving others what they want in the way they want it, people will want to be on your team. If you're a leader, they will want to follow you. People will more completely enjoy the 2,000+ hours they spend at work with you each year!

Let's take a minute now and review the Values areas you've explored in the relationships we've covered so far.

With your spouse, you explored two Values areas:

A. The Relationship with a Spouse Values area

B. The Life Values area

With your children, you explored two Values areas:

A. The Relationship with a Mom/Dad Values area

B. The Life Values area

With your friends, you explored two Values areas:

A. The Relationship with a Friend Values area

B. The Life Values area

With your work associates, you will want to explore three Values areas:

A. The Job/Occupation Values area

B. The Relationship with an Associate/Manager/Leader Values area

C. The Life Values area

THE VALUES AND SPARKS DISCOVERY PROCESS FOR A WORK RELATIONSHIP

*First, explain to your work associate **why** you want to ask these questions. Of course, the best way to do this is for both of you to study this book together.*

A. Explore the Job/Occupation Values Area.

1. Ask this Values Question: "What's most important to you in a job/occupation?" Discover his/her #1 Value for this area.

2. For the Value you discovered in Step 1 above, ask the Sparks Question, "What has to happen in order for you to feel (#1 Value)?" Discover his/her first Spark for the #1 Value.

3. Discover at least two other Sparks for his/her #1 Value by asking, "What else has to happen in order for you to feel (#1 Value)?"

4. Discover at least two other Values for the Job/Occupation Values area by asking, "What else is important to you in a job/occupation?" Then repeat Steps 2 and 3 to discover at least two Sparks for each additional Value you discover.

B. Explore the Relationship Values Area.

1. Ask this Values Question: "What's most important to you in a relationship with an associate/manager/leader?" Discover his/her #1 Value for this area.

2. For the Value you discovered in Step 1 above, ask the Sparks Question, "What has to happen in order for you to feel (#1 Value)?" Discover his/her first Spark for the #1 Value.

3. Discover at least two other Sparks for his/her #1 Value by asking, "What else has to happen in order for you to feel (#1 Value)?"

4. Discover at least two other Values for the Relationship Values area by asking, "What else is important to you in a relationship with an associate/manager/leader?" Then repeat Steps 2 and 3 to discover at least two Sparks for each additional Value you discover.

C. Explore the Life Values Area.

1. Ask this Values Question: "What's most important to you in life?" Discover his/her #1 Value for this area.

2. For the Value you discovered in Step 1 above, ask the Sparks Question, "What has to happen in order for you to feel (#1 Value)?" Discover his/her first Spark for the #1 Value.

3. Discover at least two other Sparks for his/her #1 Value by asking, "What else has to happen in order for you to feel (#1 Value)?"

4. Discover at least two other Values for the Life Values area by asking, "What else is important to you in life?" Then repeat Steps 2 and 3 to discover at least two Sparks for each additional Value you discover.

An Example of Using the Values Discovery Process with a Work Associate

The following is a composite of conversations I've had with work associates through the years.

Nate	"Brad, I really like to get to know the people I work with here at XYZ Corporation because everyone has different wants and needs. Would you mind answering a few questions?"
Brad	"Sounds good to me."
Nate	"What's most important to you in a job?"
Brad	"Oh, I don't know. Making lots of money, I guess." (A vague Spark answer)
Nate	"If you made lots of money, what would that mean to you?" (I'm asking him to think of his Value for the Spark "making lots of money.")

Brad	"That would mean I'm successful." (One of his Values. It may or may not be his highest Value.)
Nate	"How much money would you have to make this year to feel like you're successful?" (I'm getting more specific on his Spark for success.)
Brad	"$30,000."
Nate	"How much are you making now?"
Brad	"$25,000." (He's $5,000 short. I know if I can help him move toward making $30,000, I will strengthen our relationship.)
Nate	"I've got some ideas of skills you can learn that could lead to an improved income. When we have some more time, we can review a few of them."
Brad	"Great!" (People get excited when they feel understood and supported.)
Nate	"What else has to happen for you to feel success?" (I'm after his second Spark for success.)
Brad	"Hmmmm, I guess being recognized for the good work I do." (His second Spark for the Value of success.)
Nate	"There are a lot of ways to be recognized. Which ways are important to you?" (I'm getting very clear on this Spark.)

Brad   "It doesn't have to be anything formal, although that's okay. I just like to be told every once in a while that I'm doing a good job."

I could discover more Sparks for the Value of success, but I decide to move on to a second Value.

Nate   "In addition to success, what else is important to you in a job?" (I'm after a second Value in the Job Values area.)

Brad   "I want a job that challenges me." (Challenge is his second Value.)

Nate   "Of the two things you've mentioned so far—success and challenge—which one is most important to you?" (I want to discover his #1 Value. The order of a person's Values is useful information.)

Brad   "That's a good question."

Nate   "What's a good answer?"

Brad   "Probably challenge."

Nate   "How does a job have to be arranged for it to be challenging?" (Another way of asking for a Spark. It gets tiresome to always ask, "What has to happen in order for you to feel _____?")

Brad	"I need to constantly be learning." (His first Spark for challenge.)
Nate	"What are a few things you would like to learn now that would help you the most? I'll help you learn them as quickly as possible." (I want to discover how I can help him right now. When I do that, I'll have an eager and hardworking associate in my department.)
Brad	"Whoa, you'd do that for me?"
Nate	"Within reason, whenever and wherever I can."
Brad	"I need to learn that new accounting program we use here in the office."
Nate	"That's a good first choice. I'll get you enrolled in the next full-day training class. After you're done with the class, we'll talk about the next step."
Brad	"I really appreciate your time. Quite frankly, I was kind of skeptical when we first started this."
Nate	"I'm glad you like it. Sometime I'll show you how to do it if you want to."
Brad	"Let's do it."

Now I'm going to move on to the second Values area—the Relationship with an Associate/Manager/Leader. In this area, we will discover a whole new set of Values and Sparks.

Nate   "I'm curious. What's most important to you in a relationship with an associate here at work?"

Brad   (He answers very quickly and with a fair amount of intensity.) "Respect." (His first Value for this Values area.)

Nate   "That didn't take you long to answer. Did you ever work at a company where you didn't feel respected?" (I knew from the way he answered my last question that he probably had felt disrespected in a previous job.)

Brad   "You bet. I quit my last job because I wasn't given any respect."

Nate   "You sound like Rodney Dangerfield. Do you think the problem was with you, them, or both?"

Brad   "What do you mean by that?"

Nate   "Sometimes people have such unrealistic expectations of how other people should act that they're never satisfied no matter what situation they're in."

Brad   "Man, I never thought of it like that. Maybe I have been a little overboard with my expectations."

Nate   "That's just something to think about. In the meantime, what can I do to let you know you're respected?" (Another form of the Sparks Question. Remember, this whole process is much more than a series of specific questions; it's a way of thinking.)

Brad	"When you give me an assignment, don't be constantly looking over my shoulder." (He states his Spark in the negative.)
Nate	"You've told me what you don't want me to do. Tell me what you *do* want me to do."
Brad	"When you give me an assignment, let me run with it."
Nate	"Be a little more specific. What does 'Let me run with it' mean?"
Brad	"It means that you never bother me about it or ask me how I'm doing." (It looks like some of his unrealistic expectations are beginning to pop up. But better now than later. Just because somebody says that they want to be treated in a certain way doesn't mean that you must do it. As in this case, maybe it would be appropriate to educate the person a little and/or negotiate a plan that's agreeable to both of you.)
Nate	"Brad, I appreciate your independence. We need independent thinkers around here; **and** I'm responsible for the results of this department. I need to know what's going on so I can help you if I can, and coordinate the efforts of the other people in the department with what you're doing. How can we arrange it so I get the information I need, **and** you feel respected?"
Brad	"Yeah, I see what you mean. How about if I give you a written report of how I'm doing every Friday?"

Nate   "That sounds fine. I'll be expecting it each Friday. In addition, how about if I just stick my head into your office every week or so to see how you're doing? I'm not trying to be Big Brother or anything. I just want to make sure we're all moving in the same direction. And if you ever want to try something that's in a completely different direction, let me know, and I'll see what I can do. Of course, my door is always open to you if you have any questions or need some resources."

Brad   "That sounds fair." (We've negotiated the rules of the game.)

Now I would move on to discover more of his Values and Sparks for the Relationship with an Associate/Manager/Leader Values area. Then I would discover his Values and Sparks for the Life Values area.

You may have noticed by now that we always start with the least personal Values area and progressively move to more personal Values areas. In this chapter, this is the order we used:

A. the Job/Occupation Values area

B. the Relationship with an Associate/Manager/Leader Values area

C. the Life Values area

Doing it this way allows the person answering the questions to gradually "open up."

In the next week, preferably tomorrow, discover one or more of your work associates' Values and Sparks by completing the Exercises for Action on the next pages.

EXERCISES FOR ACTION

THE VALUES AND SPARKS DISCOVERY PROCESS FOR A WORK RELATIONSHIP

*First, explain to your associate **why** you want to ask these questions. Of course, the best way to do this is to study this book together. You might want to review the Additional Insights on pages 37–41. Record all of your answers in your journal or notebook.*

A. Explore the Job/Occupation Values Area.

1. Ask this Values Question: "What's most important to you in a job/occupation?" Discover his/her #1 Value for this area.

2. For the Value you discovered in Step 1 above, ask the Sparks Question, "What has to happen in order for you to feel (#1 Value)?" Discover his/her first Spark for the #1 Value.

3. Discover at least two other Sparks for his/her #1 Value by asking, "What else has to happen in order for you to feel (#1 Value)?"

4. Discover at least two other Values for the Job/Occupation Values area by asking, "What else is important to you in a job/occupation?" Then repeat Steps 2 and 3 to discover at least two Sparks for each additional Value you discover.

B. Explore the Relationship Values Area.

1. Ask this Values Question: "What's most important to you in a relationship with an associate/manager/leader?" Discover his/her #1 Value for this area.

2. For the Value you discovered in Step 1 above, ask the Sparks Question, "What has to happen in order for you to feel (#1 Value)?" Discover his/her first Spark for the #1 Value.

3. Discover at least two other Sparks for his/her #1 Value by asking, "What else has to happen in order for you to feel (#1 Value)?"

4. Discover at least two other Values for the Relationship Values area by asking, "What else is important to you in a relationship with an associate/manager/leader?" Then repeat Steps 2 and 3 to discover at least two Sparks for each additional Value you discover.

C. Explore the Life Values Area.

1. Ask this Values Question: "What's most important to you in life?" Discover his/her #1 Value for this area.

2. For the Value you discovered in Step 1 above, ask the Sparks Question, "What has to happen in order for you to feel (#1 Value)?" Discover his/her first Spark for the #1 Value.

3. Discover at least two other Sparks for his/her #1 Value by asking, "What else has to happen in order for you to feel (#1 Value)?"

4. Discover at least two other Values for the Life Values area by asking, "What else is important to you in life?" Then repeat Steps 2 and 3 to discover at least two Sparks for each additional Value you discover.

In one way or another we're all involved with influence. If you don't sell products or services, you do "sell" your ideas to others. If you have children, you "sell" them on "doing the right thing." You "sell" yourself to the people you meet every day. So it's important that everyone read and learn from the next chapter . . . **Influence Relationships.**

8

Influence
Relationships

Tell me what's wrong with the following scenario. A new female patient walks into a dental office. The dentist has never met her. Before she opens her mouth, the dentist walks up to her and says, "You need three porcelain crowns on your back teeth, complete orthodontic treatment, and two of your wisdom teeth removed." What's wrong with the scene is obvious. The dentist would be prescribing a course of action before he/she did an examination and diagnosis, and **prescription without diagnosis is malpractice.** The patient would probably turn around and walk out of the office, and the dentist would eventually have his/her license taken away!

Prescription without diagnosis is malpractice.

In my experience of working with thousands of salespeople, the majority of them do something similar to our clueless dentist. *They don't do a thorough diagnosis by accurately discovering the prospect's Values and Sparks.* Then, they make things worse by doing one of the following: One, they sell everyone the same way by merely telling the prospect a list of their product's or service's features and hoping that one or more of the features excite the prospect. This is the "spray and pray" approach to sales! Or two, they sell through **their own** Values and Sparks. They think what they believe is important about their product/service is what the prospect should believe is important.

Every product or service has a list of features that prospects could desire. But it is vital that you remember this: **A feature is not a benefit unless the feature gives prospects their Values according to their set of Sparks!**

The truly great influencers don't make the above mistakes. They've learned to discover what people want, how they want it, and then they link these desires to their product or service. This is

Elegant Influence. In Chapter 3, you met my friend and his limousine service. Before he attended my program, he was an honest and hardworking guy. He truly cared about people and probably gave better than average service. He lacked one skill, however, a skill that almost caused him to lose his business. He hadn't learned the four steps of Elegant Influence that would effectively influence people to take action and purchase his services.

◆

A feature is not a benefit unless the feature gives prospects their Values according to their set of Sparks!

◆

THE FOUR ELEGANT INFLUENCE STEPS

1. Elegant Influencers realize that people don't really want your product or service. They want what your product or service will do for them. That is, *people want a product or service because it will give them the unique set of emotions (Values) they desire most in the way they want it (Sparks).*

   Here's a partial list of the possible emotions people desire from a product or service:

a. **Success**—They want to be seen as successful in their personal and business lives and have the rewards of success.

b. **Admiration**—They want to stand out in their personal life or their company.

c. **Intelligence**—They want to make the "right" choice. They want others to view them as educated.

d. **Security**—They don't want to take a chance. At one time in the business world, there was a saying, "Nobody ever got fired for buying IBM." IBM was the safe, secure choice. Of course, people also want security on a personal level, which is why "location, location, location" is what's most important in a home choice for many folks.

e. **Freedom**—They (like me) want to be relieved of unnecessary work and be able to do the things they desire.

f. **Belonging**—They want a close relationship with you and your company. They want to be part of your family. They want a Saturn car so they can go to the picnic in Spring Hill, Tennessee every summer.

g. **Uniqueness**—They want to be different from everyone else.

h. **Trust**—They want to know that you and your company will always be there for them. People don't want to put their money in Fred's Bank. The feeling of trust seems a little lacking there. They want to put their money in a place with a name like First Worldwide Trust Bank.

i. **Adventure**—They want a thrill. Nissan knows this. In 1997 and 1998, their slogan was "Life's an adventure! Enjoy the ride!"

2. Elegant Influencers know that a certain set of factors must be present for people to feel their Values. These are their *Sparks.*

3. Elegant Influencers discover people's Values and Sparks in two Values areas and, if the relationship is close enough, in a third Values area. They:

a. discover the Values and Sparks that may be connected to their *product or service.*

b. discover the Values and Sparks that may be connected to their *relationship with you and your company.*

c. if appropriate, discover people's Values and Sparks in *life.*

4. Elegant Influencers *only promote the features of their product or service that match people's Values and Sparks.* This will keep people focused on what's truly important and will decrease objections. Many objections are created when you tell people features that don't match their Values and Sparks.

THE VALUES AND SPARKS DISCOVERY PROCESS FOR AN INFLUENCE RELATIONSHIP

*First, be certain that you have established trust and rapport with the person. Then explain why you **want** to ask these questions. Say something like, "Mike, I really want to get to know my clients because everyone has different wants and needs. Would you mind answering a few questions so I can discover what's most important to you?"*

A. Explore the Product/Service Values Area.

1. Ask this Values Question: "What's most important to you in (your kind of product or service)?" Discover his/her #1 Value for this area.

2. For the Value you discovered in Step 1 above, ask the Sparks Question, "What has to happen in order for you to feel (#1 Value)?" Discover his/her first Spark for the #1 Value.

3. Discover at least two other Sparks for his/her #1 Value by asking, "What else has to happen in order for you to feel (#1 Value)?"

4. Discover at least two other Values for the Product/ Service Values area by asking, "What else is important to you in (your kind of product or service)?" Then repeat Steps 2 and 3 to discover at least two Sparks for each additional Value you discover.

B. Explore the Relationship Values Area.

1. Ask this Values Question: "What's most important to you in a relationship with (the word or phrase that best describes your relationship)?" Discover his/her #1 Value for this area.

2. For the Value you discovered in Step 1 above, ask the Sparks Question, "What has to happen in order for you to feel (#1 Value)?" OR "What would my company and I have to do in order for you to feel (#1 Value)?" Discover his/her first Spark for the #1 Value.

3. Discover at least two other Sparks for his/her #1 Value by asking, "What else has to happen in order for you to feel (#1 Value)?" OR "What else would my company and I have to do in order for you to feel (#1 Value)?"

4. Discover at least two other Values for the Relationship Values area by asking, "What else is important to you in a relationship with (the word or phrase that best describes your relationship)?" Then repeat Steps 2 and 3 to discover at least two Sparks for each additional Value you discover.

C. If your product/service has a significant influence on an individual's personal life, explore the Life Values Area.

1. Ask this Values Question: "What's most important to you in life?" Discover his/her #1 Value for this area.

2. For the Value you discovered in Step 1, ask the Sparks Question, "What has to happen in order for you to feel (#1 Value)?" Discover his/her first Spark for the #1 Value.

3. Discover at least two other Sparks for his/her #1 Value by asking, "What else has to happen in order for you to feel (#1 Value)?"

4. Discover at least two other Values for the Life Values area by asking, "What else is important to you in life?" Then repeat Steps 2 and 3 to discover at least two Sparks for each additional Value you discover.

I call the Values and Sparks Discover Questions **"Triple Impact"** because they do the following three things:

1. Triple Impact Questions *develop rapport.* They let people know that I'm interested in their unique desires. People need to be understood before they will want to understand what you have to offer.

2. Triple Impact Questions *put people into a positive emotional state.* When this happens, your products/ services, your company, and you become linked to that state. This is what happened to my friend who owned the limousine service. He asked the woman on the phone the Triple Impact Questions. She answered them and talked about the wild, crazy, outrageous evening she wanted. How did she feel in the moment? Wild,

crazy, and outrageous. Who got connected to that feeling via the phone line? My friend! Who is the lady going to select for her limo ride? You guessed it.

When it comes right down to it, you're not a salesperson. You're a state inducer! You get paid to induce states in people so that they take action and buy your products and services. The next time someone asks you what you do for a living, you can say, "I'm a state inducer." That will get the conversation going.

Remember the Dancing Raisins? Their commercials were "state inducers" for the California Raisin Growers. You watch the commercial, you feel good, you link the good feelings to raisins. You want more of the good feelings, so you go out and buy raisins to achieve them. Simple, yet profound.

You're the Dancing Raisin of your product, service, or idea. This isn't as silly as it sounds. Do you have customers/clients who are genuinely glad to see you when you walk into a room? Most people do. That indicates that you're a Dancing Raisin to those people. How tough of a sale are these clients? Most people answer, "Easy!" Why? Because these clients are feeling a positive emotion that is conducive to agreement and action.

3. Triple Impact Questions *give you valuable information* so that you can show people how they can get exactly what they want in the way they want it, through your products and services. Precision is power!

When you ask Triple Impact Questions, don't grill people by asking a rapid-fire series of questions. Most folks will become resistant if they feel pushed, or if they feel you're going to use the information against them. If, however, they feel you have their best interests at heart, if you verbally and nonverbally communicate that you care about them, they will open up and tell you information that will empower both of you. Occasionally, you will have to slow people down because they will tell you more than you need to know! As you ask the Triple Impact Questions, be a partner in exploring challenges and opportunities.

If you feel the person becoming a little defensive, back off. Be like a great boxer and "bob and weave" as you discover the information. Get a little bit of information, then talk about something else for a while. Then discover some more information. You can even discover the information over a series of appointments. **Remember, discovering Values and Sparks is more a way of thinking (i.e., what do they want and how do they want it) than a series of questions.**

An Example of the Values Discovery Process in an Influence Situation

In the past week, I made a sale to a financial institution to create and deliver a comprehensive "Elegant Influence" training program to all their employees. My competition was three companies who had extensive experience with this type of client. I had never created a comprehensive training program for any financial institution! After I made the sale, I asked the person to whom I made the sale to tell me why he chose me. He said, "The committee and I felt you understood our situation completely. You know what we want from our training program, and we feel that you were the best person to provide it for us."

Here's an edited version of how our first conversation went. Incidentally, the best influencers don't *talk to* people. They have *conversations with* people.

Nate   "Ted, I really want to get to know the people I'm going to do training with" (How's that for assuming the sale?) "because all companies are different, and they all have a unique set of needs. Would you mind answering a few questions so I can learn about your credit union?"

Ted   "Let 'er fly."

Nate	"What's most important to you in a training program?"
Ted	"I want a training program that produces results. We need to help our people become more proactive in suggesting various services to our members. If the members don't get their financial services from us, they're going to get them from someone else." (Notice that he says he wants results. Technically speaking, results isn't a Value because it isn't an emotion. To him, results is the same as success, which is an emotion. In this situation, I'm going to stay with his word as a Value because that's how he defines success.)
Nate	"What kind of results will you have to get in order to know the training program has been successful?" (I merge results and success as I ask for his Sparks.)
Ted	"Well, a successful program would get our people to be proactive. Right now, they just wait for people to ask for services. We want to get them to take the initiative and influence our members to use our services."
Nate	"Good. What other results will you have to get in order to know the training program has been successful?" (I ask for a second Spark.)

Ted	"Our people would consistently do a few of the little things right." (He gives me a vague Spark. I need to get clarity.)
Nate	"What are those little things?"
Ted	"The first would be to smile when they greet people. The second would be to say the person's name at least three times during the conversation. The third would be to always have their name badge on so the member knows their name. The fourth would be to listen so they can discover people's needs."
Nate	"Great, we will definitely include these and any other little things we find in the Discovery Phase of the program."
Ted	"Sounds good to me!"
Nate	"In addition to results, what else is important to you in a training program?" (I'm after his second Value for the Program Value area.)
Ted	"We want our people to be involved." (His second Value is involvement.)
Nate	"What do you mean by involved?" (When it comes to influence, clarity is power.)
Ted	"I want an action plan at the end of each exercise so that the people can put into action the information they've learned in the training program" (Spark #1).

"I want the training program to be spaced through time. Maybe we have two half-days of training with seven or ten days between them. Then people can put their learning into action in the real world and talk about how it went at the second session" (Spark #2). "I want our people to commit to making some changes in behavior" (Spark #3). "I want to be able to monitor the change in behavior" (Spark #4). (As you can tell, I'm writing like crazy!)

Next, I went on to discover two more Values for the Training Program Value area and the Sparks that went with them. Finally, I progressed to his Values in a Relationship with a Training Organization.

Nate   "What's most important to you in a relationship with a training organization?"

Ted   "I like your questions." (You will get this comment frequently.) "What's most important to me in a relationship with a training company is that they listen to us and create a program that fits our needs. We have a unique situation here, and it's going to take a customized program to achieve our objectives." (His #1 Value is the feeling of being understood.)

Nate   "It sounds like being understood is very important to you. Have you ever had an experience with a training organization where you weren't understood?" (Sometimes it is very helpful to understand the pain the company has experienced in the past, so that you won't create a repeat performance in the future.)

Ted   "You bet we have! We once had a training company come in here and do a canned program even though they said it would be customized. It didn't go well at all."

Nate   "We'll make sure the program we do for you will be customized and effective. If you choose, you can be involved in the creation of the program and approve it every step of the way. How does that sound?" (I'm getting his approval and asking for a small commitment.)

Ted   "Sounds great to me!"

Nate   "We really want to understand you so that we can create a customized program for you. What process should we go through to make that happen?" (A form of a Sparks Question)

Ted   "Today has been an excellent start. I'll need a formal proposal from you within seven days. I'll even coach you in preparing the proposal. Next, we should schedule a meeting with the selection committee to get them familiar with you and your training program. Then, our committee will make a decision by the end of the month." (Things are looking positive! He's telling me the company's buying strategy—the steps they go through to make a decision—and he will champion me with the selection committee.)

I ended the Values and Sparks Discovery Process by discovering two more Values in a Relationship with a Training Organization Values area and the Sparks that went with them. Because my corporate training program didn't have a significant impact on Ted's personal life, I didn't explore the Life Values area.

The Values and Sparks Discovery Process only takes a few minutes and there is no better way to spend 3–30 minutes with a customer/client. Notice how questions control the conversation. You often hear that great salespeople talk about 20% of the time and listen about 80% of the time. I believe this is true. What isn't well known is that great salespeople listen to "the right stuff" because they ask the right questions. The "right stuff" is vital information about people's needs and desires that you can use to help them get what they want in the way they want it.

Just as a diamond has many facets, the application of the Diamond Touch has many facets, too. In this chapter, you learned about the influence facet. Put your learning to work right now by completing the Exercises for Action on the following pages.

EXERCISES FOR ACTION

THE VALUES AND SPARKS DISCOVERY PROCESS FOR AN INFLUENCE RELATIONSHIP

*First, explain to your customer/client **why** you want to ask these questions. You might want to review the Additional Insights on pages 37–41. Record all of your answers in your journal or notebook.*

A. Explore the Product/Service Values Area.

1. Ask this Values Question: "What's most important to you in (your kind of product or service)?" Discover his/her #1 Value for this area.

2. For the Value you discovered in Step 1 above, ask the Sparks Question, "What has to happen in order for you to feel (#1 Value)?" Discover his/her first Spark for the #1 Value.

3. Discover at least two other Sparks for his/her #1 Value by asking, "What else has to happen in order for you to feel (#1 Value)?"

4. Discover at least two other Values for the Product/ Service Values area by asking, "What else is important to you in (your kind of product or service)?" Then repeat Steps 2 and 3 to discover at least two Sparks for each additional Value you discover.

B. Explore the Relationship Values Area.

1. Ask this Values Question: "What's most important to you in a relationship with (the word or phrase that best describes your relationship)?" Discover his/her #1 Value for this area.

2. For the Value you discovered in Step 1 above, ask the Sparks Question, "What has to happen in order for you to feel (#1 Value)?" OR "What would my company and I have to do in order for you to feel (#1 Value)?" Discover his/her first Spark for the #1 Value.

3. Discover at least two other Sparks for his/her #1 Value by asking, "What else has to happen in order for you to feel (#1 Value)?" OR "What else would my company and I have to do in order for you to feel (#1 Value)?"

4. Discover at least two other Values for the Relationship Values area by asking, "What else is important to you in a relationship with (the word or phrase that best describes your relationship)?" Then repeat Steps 2 and 3 to discover at least two Sparks for each additional Value you discover.

C. If your product/service has a significant influence on an individual's personal life, explore the Life Values Area.

1. Ask this Values Question: "What's most important to you in life?" Discover his/her #1 Value for this area.

2. For the Value you discovered in Step 1 above, ask the Sparks Question, "What has to happen in order for you to feel (#1 Value)?" Discover his/her first Spark for the #1 Value.

3. Discover at least two other Sparks for his/her #1 Value by asking, "What else has to happen in order for you to feel (#1 Value)?"

4. Discover at least two other Values for the Life Values area by asking, "What else is important to you in life?" Then repeat Steps 2 and 3 to discover at least two Sparks for each additional Value you discover.

The Values and Sparks Discovery Process will not only help you **make** the sale, it will help you **keep** your customers by giving them the exact products and services they desire. To learn more about this vital skill, read the next chapter . . . **Service Relationships**.

9

Service
Relationships

The average American corporation loses half of its customers every five years. Most studies show that more than half of the customers leave because of poor service, not because of products or price.

Think of a time when you experienced poor service. What Value of yours wasn't met? What did the service provider do to break your rules? What *could* have been done to give you what you wanted in the way you wanted it in that situation? Write your answers in your journal or notebook.

Nowhere does the Diamond Rule come more into play than in servicing your customers/clients. Anyone who has been in the service industry for more than a day knows that different people want their service in *their* way. Levi's has done extremely well with their custom-fit jeans. They provide you with a kit to measure yourself. You then use the Internet to send your measurements to the factory where a pair of custom jeans is made for you from a computer-generated pattern. You receive your jeans within two weeks. Custom Foot, a shoe store chain, allows you to design your own custom-fit shoe. You go to their store, pick the style and color of shoe you desire, and have your foot measured by a three-dimensional scanner. The information is sent via the Internet to a factory in Italy, where your shoes are made. You receive them in three weeks.

I recently had a personal experience that exemplified Diamond Touch service. I had just landed at the Tampa airport. I collected my luggage and headed out to hail a cab. A cab pulled up and out bounced a man by the name of Herb. He cheerfully greeted me, introduced himself, and placed my luggage in his trunk. He noticed my heavy-duty, fold-up metal luggage carrier and said, "I have a client who really needs one of these. Would you mind if I get the manufacturer's name and phone number off your cart?"

I said, "Sure," as I was thinking, "This guy is really different!" I slid into the back seat of an extremely clean, but not overly fancy car. I noticed that he had several newspapers and a box of Kleenex neatly arranged on the area behind the seat. In the front seat, he had a cooler full of different kinds of juices. Beside the cooler was a box loaded with snacks. He offered me a juice and a snack. I gladly accepted.

I told him, "Boy, you really have this baby loaded with goodies, don't you?"

He responded, "It's my pleasure to make your trip as enjoyable as possible. Would you like to listen to a particular kind of music, or would you like to view a video that will acquaint you with the Tampa/St. Pete area?" He had a video player and small TV mounted on his dashboard.

As we talked more, I learned that he was known by almost everyone in the area as the Juice Man. He had hundreds of regular, loyal customers who enjoyed his unique brand of Diamond Touch service. As we pulled up to the hotel, he gave me his card and said, "If you're ever in Tampa again, I'd be honored to serve you."

Then he asked this question: "Is there anything I can do next time to make your trip even more enjoyable?" I've purchased a dozen cars in my lifetime and no car salesperson has ever asked me that question. I've bought three houses in my lifetime and no real estate professional has ever asked me that question. I've gone to four dentists in my lifetime and no one in the dental office has ever asked me that question. **A cab driver was the first one to ask me that question!**

I've got three questions for you:

1. How much did the juice and snack I ate cost him— maybe a dollar?

2. How big of a tip did I give him—considerably more than a dollar?

3. Do I call him every time I come to Tampa? You bet. He can't always pick me up, and if he can't, he has one of his friends do it.

If a guy in a cab can consistently offer Diamond Touch service, do you think your company and you can, too? You know the answer to that one!

In some service situations, where you're servicing mass numbers of people and/or you don't have much time to talk with them, you will want to use the Golden Rule: Serve others in the way you would like to be served.

In the following three service situations, however, you will want to give Diamond Touch service—serve others in the unique way they would like to be served.

1. With all your best current accounts. You will want this information to serve them even better than you are now.

2. When a new service account comes on board. This is the perfect time to ask, before there are any challenges.

3. Whenever you're experiencing a challenge with a current account. If there's a challenge, it means you're breaking one or more of their rules!

THE VALUES AND SPARKS DISCOVERY PROCESS FOR A SERVICE RELATIONSHIP

*First, explain to your customer/client **why** you want to ask these questions. You will only need to explore one Values area when it comes to service.*

1. Ask this Values Question: "What's most important to you in the service you receive from a vendor?" (If appropriate, you may want to use another word than *vendor.*) Discover his/her #1 Value for this area.

2. For the Value you discovered in Step 1 above, ask the Sparks Question, "What has to happen in order for you to feel (#1 Value)?" OR, "What would my company and I have to do in order for you to feel (#1 Value)?" Discover his/her first Spark for the #1 Value.

3. Discover at least two other Sparks for his/her #1 Value by asking, "What else has to happen in order for you to feel (#1 Value)?" OR, "What else would my company and I have to do in order for you to feel (#1 Value)?"

4. Discover at least two other Values by asking, "What else is important to you in the service you receive from a vendor?" Then repeat Steps 2 and 3 to discover at least two Sparks for each additional Value you discover.

An Example of the Values Discovery Process in a Service Relationship

You may have noticed that the lines between sales and service are blurring these days. Many salespeople are servicing accounts and many service people are being asked to sell additional services to their customers/clients. Our example in this chapter will be one where a service provider discovers a customer need by asking the Service Values Questions.

Chloe	"Bill, I've been servicing your account for three years now. I think I've been doing a pretty good job, but I'd like to do even better. Would you mind answering a few questions so I can discover with more accuracy the kind of service you truly desire?"
Bill	"I'd be glad to."
Chloe	"What are the most important things we are doing right now to give you great service? Maybe we can do them even better." (Remember, I said that this whole Values and Sparks Discovery Process is more than just a series of questions. It's a way of thinking that basically says, "What do they want and how do they want it?" Chloe knows Bill wants great service. She's going right for the Sparks that ignite great service for him.)

Bill	"98% of the time you do your service right the first time." (His first Spark for great service.)
Chloe	"What's the next most important thing we're doing to give you great service?"
Bill	"You're really quick. Most of the time, when something goes wrong, you're here within three hours. We need that."
Chloe	"Is there anything we can be doing better when it comes to service for you?" (The Juice Man Question—maybe there is a Spark missing in the relationship.)
Bill	"I know this isn't your fault, Chloe. But our machine seems to be breaking down more than it should." (Chloe has discovered a pain that needs some attention. This pain can't be fixed with all the service in the world, but the new XKE Model that just came out is much more reliable.)
Chloe	"You're in luck, Bill! We've just come out with a new XKE Model that is much more reliable. Can I have Bud come over tomorrow and show it to you?"
Bill	"You bet!" (The sale is 50% made now!)

Customization is an extremely important concept in business as we head into the next millennium. People want custom fitted jeans, and Levi Strauss is delivering. People want choices when it comes to ice cream, and Ben & Jerry's is delivering with Cherry Garcia and Chubby Hubby. People want customized service. Are *you* going to deliver it with a Diamond Touch?

EXERCISES FOR ACTION

THE VALUES AND SPARKS DISCOVERY PROCESS FOR A SERVICE RELATIONSHIP

*First, explain to your customer/client **why** you want to ask these questions. You might want to review the Additional Insights on pages 37–41. Record all of your answers in your journal or notebook. You will only need to explore one Values area when it comes to service.*

1. Ask this Values Question: "What's most important to you in the service you receive from a vendor?" Discover his/her #1 Value for this area.

2. For the Value you discovered in Step 1 above, ask the Sparks Question, "What has to happen in order for you to feel (#1 Value)?" OR, "What would my company and I have to do in order for you to feel (#1 Value)?" Discover his/her first Spark for the #1 Value.

3. Discover at least two other Sparks for his/her #1 Value by asking, "What else has to happen in order for you to feel (#1 Value)?" OR, "What else would my company and I have to do in order for you to feel (#1 Value)?"

4. Discover at least two other Values by asking, "What else is important to you in the service you receive from a vendor?" Then repeat Steps 2 and 3 to discover at least two Sparks for each additional Value you discover.

Can you see how knowing the Values and Sparks of the people who are most important to you makes all the difference in your relationships? What if you could get at least a general idea of the values of every person you meet? You'll learn how in Section 3...

3

The Values Groups

In the last Section, you learned the questions you need to ask to discover a person's unique set of Values and Sparks in six different kinds of relationships: husband/wife, parent/child, friendships, work relationships, influence relationships, and service relationships. With the Values and Sparks Discovery Process, you can learn a tremendous amount of information in a relatively short period of time. It does take some time, however. In some relationships, you don't have the time to do the process.

That's why the information in this Section is so important. In the next five chapters, you will learn about five different groups of people. Each group shares a common set of Values and Sparks. Because each group shares a common set of Values ("Here's what I want") and Sparks ("Here's how I want it"), understanding these five groups and how to quickly determine which group a person belongs to gives you the power to give them what they really want with a fair degree of accuracy—much higher than just guessing.

The information in this Section is based on the Values and Lifestyle Survey (VALS). The initial research on VALS was done by the Stanford Research Institute in the 1970s. In 1978, VALS was introduced to the world and embraced by several marketing and advertising companies. They knew that if manufacturers could use intelligent and targeted marketing and advertising to connect their products/services to the Values of a huge group of people, that group would want to buy the product/service to give them those emotions they wanted most.

VALS is technically called a "psychographic segmentation system." It divides (segments) a population based on psychographics. You are probably familiar with demographics—the age, income, education, sex, and other social characteristics of a population. Psychographics refer to the opinions, beliefs, and emotions that drive behavior.

VALS is periodically revised and updated. I've simplified the VALS information in a way that will make it more understandable and useful to you.

Take a look at the titles of the following five chapters:

- Popcorn & Picnics
- Cars & Bars
- Polos & Porsches
- Degrees & Dolphins
- Red Dog & Rodmans

Each chapter title is a pair of things, animals, or people the group values highly. Are you getting an idea of what each group is like just by seeing the pair of words? I hope so. Be prepared to be thoroughly amused and fascinated by the information you're about to learn. After you read this section, you will never look at another television commercial or another person the same.

Please remember that while we're dealing with generalizations here, the information you're about to learn is a verified and valid set of assumptions that can help you give people what they really want with a higher degree of accuracy than you are now.

Please remember, whenever you can, ask people their Values and Sparks.

You will probably notice that I poke some good-natured fun at each of the groups. Each group has its unique set of foibles and idiosyncrasies that are easy and healthy to laugh at!

10

Popcorn & Picnics

Mary is a manager in a large Midwestern bank. She's on the fast track to a high-level leadership position. However, in her current job as manager of a group of tellers, she's struggling. Her people work hard, but don't seem to be as interested in success as she is. She cares about her people and wants them to advance to higher positions in the bank, too. She buys them motivational tapes, but nobody wants to listen to them. Her high energy and "gung-ho" style are turning people off. She even heard through the grapevine that she is not considered a "people person." Mary is worried. To her it seems that the tellers are from another planet. In many ways, she's right. Mary is an "alien" dealing with a Values Group called Popcorn & Picnics.

GROUP OVERVIEW

Popcorn & Picnics is the largest Values Group. It's composed of traditional Americans. They work hard and are proud of it. You'll often hear them say, "We work hard and play hard." They're proud of their country (they love to fly the American flag) and their communities. They attend church every week and they always vote. They revere "family values" and tend to resist change. They may talk about "the good old days" a lot. Popcorn & Picnics tend to live in the Midwest and South, although most communities have a Popcorn & Picnics section of town.

They are all ages, because if you are brought up as a Popcorn & Picnics, you will tend to stay one your entire life. (You can take the child off the farm, but you can't take the farm out of the child.) Names tend to be passed down from generation to generation. I'm Nathaniel the fifth. My wife Barbara Dawn has the same first name as her mom. Sometimes, girls are even named after their fathers (Roberta, Rhae Jean).

PRIMARY VALUE

Popcorn & Picnics' Primary Value (the emotion they want most) is *belonging.* They deeply want to belong to groups, especially their family group. Popcorn & Picnics tend to stay in the area where they were born so they can be near their "roots." They also love to belong to clubs such as Rotary, Kiwanis, Lions, and Knights of Columbus.

◆

Popcorn & Picnics' Primary Value is *belonging*.

◆

PRIMARY SPARKS

Their Primary Sparks (what has to happen for them to feel like they belong) are #1—Getting Together, and #2—Loyal Action.

Primary Spark #1—Getting Together

What do Popcorn & Picnics do when someone in their extended family (grandma, grandpa, mom, dad, aunts, uncles, cousins, brothers, sisters, children) has a birthday? They get together. What do they do when a couple has an anniversary? They get together. What do they do when someone graduates from grade school, junior high school, high school, or college? They get together. What do they do on every holiday ever invented? They get together. Where do they go in the summer when they get together? On a picnic, of course, where everyone can play and talk. And what's their favorite food in the winter when they show the home movies of last year's vacation at Lake Okoboji, Iowa? (My entire family has gone there every summer for the last 49 years!) Popcorn, of course.

Popcorn & Picnics love to join clubs so they can (you guessed it!) get together with their friends. They may even have a bar where they regularly go, because at your "home" bar "everybody knows your name" and say, "Hey, Norm," when you walk in. They may even have a shiny silver jacket with the name of their home bar printed proudly on the back. When their favorite high school, college, or pro sports team loses a game, who lost? "WE did!" Are you beginning to get an idea of who Popcorn & Picnics are? Are any faces popping into your mind?

Primary Spark #2—Loyal Action

Popcorn & Picnics support each other (they are friends for life), their favorite athletic teams (the Chicago Cubs, for example), their favorite stock car driver (Jeff Elliott is an idol to many) through thick and thin. They love to attend high school homecomings ("Be true to your school") or Independence Day parades ("Don't go burning any American flags around here"). The University of Nebraska Cornhuskers and the Pittsburgh Steelers sell tons of officially licensed clothing to Popcorn & Picnics so they can show their team loyalty. Who would wear a wedge of foam cheese on their head to display their loyalty to their beloved Green Bay Packers? Popcorn & Picnics, that's who! How's this for loyalty: Kids in Green Bay loan their bikes to the Packer players so they can ride from the practice field to the locker room!

PSYCHIC WOUND

A Psychic Wound is **the pain a particular Values Group will do almost anything to avoid.** Popcorn & Picnics' Psychic Wound is *being separated.* When you can "heal" someone's Psychic Wound and show them how to keep it healed, your relationship with them will be enhanced. When your product or service can heal people's Psychic Wounds, they will want to buy.

◆

A Psychic Wound is the pain a particular Values Group will do almost anything to avoid.

◆

AT&T used the power of Psychic Wounds to create their "Reach Out and Touch Someone" TV commercials. Because of their occupations and marriages, some Popcorn & Picnics are separated from their families. AT&T created the "Reach Out and Touch Someone" commercials to show them how they could heal their Psychic Wound with a long-distance call. In some areas of the country, those commercials ran for over 15 years! They must have worked.

PREFERRED CARS

Popcorn & Picnics will drive any car that is Made in America—Chevy, "The Heartbeat of America"; Ford Pickup Trucks, "Built Tough" for people who actually work for a living; Chrysler Corporation minivans so they can take the whole family on a picnic and have room for the dog who is part of the family. They hate foreign vehicles because it's not patriotic to buy one. "Damn it, if you buy a BMW, you're putting American workers out of their jobs!"

FAVORITE SOFT DRINK

Their preferred soft drink is Coke. "My granddaddy drank Coke. My daddy drinks Coke. I'm drinking Coke." The Coke slogan in 1998 is "Always Coca-Cola." What images does Coke put in their commercials? Getting together images—a happy family having a picnic in the park, or a group of children from different countries on a hillside in Greece.

Remember when Coke changed their formula? They did that because six out of ten Coke drinkers preferred the new formula in blind taste tests. But what do Popcorn & Picnics think of change? They hate it. So they went on strike and wouldn't buy any Coke products until "You bring back my original Coke!" Coke saw the light and brought back Coke Classic for Popcorn & Picnics, and continued to produce New Coke for the "New Generation" group.

FAVORITE TELEVISION PROGRAMS

Popcorn & Picnics watch "quality family programming" on the Family Channel or the Disney Channel. Popcorn & Picnics love sports so they watch cable channels like ESPN frequently. Would they rather watch *Home Improvement* or *Frasier*? *Home Improvement*, of course, with the nice family of mom, dad, and the three boys, friendly neighbors, and family pictures on the refrigerator.

Another favorite is *America's Funniest Home Videos* ("Those babies and cats are so cute!"). If you don't like those fishing and hunting shows on ESPN on Saturday morning, ("Wow, Wes, you've just caught yourself a big bass there, little buddy!"), this just shows that you're not a Popcorn & Picnics.

ADVERTISEMENTS DIRECTED TOWARD THEM

You can tell Popcorn & Picnics ads because they will have a family or getting together theme. The Kmart ads with best friends Penny Marshall and Rosie O'Donnell. ("We love Rosie's talk show . . . she's so nice.") The Budweiser Frogs ads—three buddy frogs hanging around their "home bar" trying to get some Bud. The Quaker Oats ads with Wilford Brimley—the old, chubby guy from the movie *Cocoon*. What's Wilford doing in the commercial? He's just hanging around the supermarket in the aisle next to the hearty Quaker Oats cereal in its traditional round container. Then he looks into the camera and says to you, "You should eat Quaker Oats Cereal because it's the right thing to do." This appeals to Popcorn & Picnics because they have a strong sense of right and wrong. "None of this fuzzy-wuzzy, 'do whatever you want,' Southern California stuff!"

Another hard core Popcorn & Picnics TV ad is the one for Saturn cars where Julie buys a Saturn and gets her picture put on the dealership's bulletin board with all the other Saturn owners. When Julie picks up her car, her friendly sales consultant hands her the keys and says, "This is Julie, and this is her first new car," as the other sales consultants form a circle around Julie and applaud. She is now eligible to attend the annual Saturn owners' picnic in Spring Hill, Tennessee.

Popcorn & Picnics don't want to spend a whole lot of money on lodging when they're on vacation with the kids, the in-laws, and the dog, so they're attracted to the Motel 6 commercials with plainspoken Tom Beaudette as he says, "We'll leave the light on for ya."

How about this one? Bob is driving his Buick Le Sabre down a highway on a rainy evening. His two kids, Bobbie, Jr. and Roberta, are asleep in the back seat. A big truck passes by in the opposite direction and his wife, Ann, wakes up for an instant and smiles lovingly at Bob as the music in the background plays *Stand By Me*. This commercial will end up in the Popcorn & Picnics Hall of Fame!

PREFERRED CLOTHING AND CLOTHING STORES

Popcorn & Picnics don't spend a whole lot of money on clothes. Because they tend to have large families and the brothers and sisters tend to live near each other, hand-me-downs are common. Their clothing is very basic—no wild colors, nothing extravagant. They don't spend money on designer clothing. It's a waste of money. They buy Levi's or Lee jeans costing no more than $20 a pair. Popcorn & Picnics wear a lot of tee shirts, sweatshirts, and jackets with the name of their favorite rock group, stock car driver, or athletic team or club printed on the front and back.

These people are the Kmart, Target, and Wal-Mart shoppers of the world, or they will shop at a friend's small neighborhood store. They love sales and "blue light specials."

TYPICAL BUMPER STICKER

"AMERICA—LOVE IT OR LEAVE IT!"

FAVORITE BEERS

Now that you have an excellent idea of who the Popcorn & Picnics are, what kind of beer do you think they drink? An expensive import lager? An exclusive and unusual microbrewed beer? Hardly. These people want their Budweiser and lots of it! What color is the Budweiser can—teal and plum? No way, Jose, Popcorn

& Picnics want red, white, and blue. What scenes do you see in a Budweiser commercial? A bunch of 35-year-old guys playing touch football in the park. They're playing hard, drinking hard, and kidding around with each other because they're "proud to be your Bud!"

There are numerous Popcorn & Picnics beers because they drink a lot of it—Miller beer (a good old American macrobrew that's brewed in a vat the size of Rhode Island). "When that whistle blows at five o'clock after a tough day at work, what time is it? It's Miller time!" Or they drink Pabst Blue Ribbon or Old Milwaukee.

HERE'S WHAT POPCORN & PICNICS ARE LIKELY TO WANT IN A RELATIONSHIP WITH YOU:

Husband/Wife Relationships

Popcorn & Picnics want to spend time with you—alone and with the family. Birthdays, anniversaries, graduations, and holidays are very important to them. They want to talk, be around, and do things with you and the kids. They want you to be there for them and be extremely loyal.

Parent/Child Relationships

Popcorn & Picnics want to connect with you. If they live with you, they want "quality time" with you and lots of it. Adult

Popcorn & Picnics want to attend their kids' baseball games, dance recitals, and school programs. If your parents live away from you, they want numerous cards, phone calls, and visits from you.

Friendships

Popcorn & Picnics want close friendships. They may even affectionately call you "Sister, Brother, Mom, Dad, Son, Daughter, Aunt, or Uncle," even if they aren't actually related to you. They want to talk to you on the phone almost every day for at least a half hour.

They want to do things with you at least once a week. They may want to go on a trip with you and your family at least once a year. They want close, loyal friendships.

Work Relationships

Remember the story at the beginning of this chapter about Popcorn & Picnics in the workplace? Remember how Mary was having trouble motivating her team? Well, Popcorn & Picnics' jobs are not what's most important to them. Their families are. They will work hard on the job because, as Wilford Brimley says, "It's the right thing to do." They may work long hours on the job if they need to buy something for the family. If you're the co-worker or a manager of a Popcorn & Picnics, they'll want to "chit-chat" with you a little each day about personal or family topics. They want to connect with you and get to know you as a person. They may want time off to attend a school conference, a softball game, or to be with a sick relative. They may ask you to attend their son's high school graduation, even if you don't know them well. It's important that you go if possible.

Sales Relationships

When selling to any Values Group, think, "How can I provide them with their Values and heal their Psychic Wounds?" Popcorn & Picnics' Primary Value is *belonging*. As a result, their relationship with you and your company may be more important to them than your product or service. A trusting and loyal relationship is extremely important to any Popcorn & Picnics. ("Like a good neighbor, State Farm is there.") They may want a lot of "small talk" in the beginning of the relationship. It will probably take more time to establish a relationship with a Popcorn & Picnics, but when you do have it established, it will last a long time.

Their Psychic Wound is *being separated*. This means that you need to say in contact with them on a regular basis. If your product or service can bring them together with the people they care about, they will want to buy.

Service Relationships

Personal service is very important to Popcorn & Picnics. They want to get to know you and want you to get to know them so that "You can be part of our team here at XYZ Corporation."

They want to see you every once in a while. They want you to care about them as a person, "not treat me like a number."

Here's a story that truly epitomizes what it means to be a Popcorn & Picnics. It's from an article in the *Wall Street Journal* entitled "Richard Evans Is an Eternal Presence on KMOX Radio." KMOX is the #1 rated news/talk radio station in St. Louis (a heavy-duty Popcorn & Picnics community). The pride of the station is Richard Evans' homey "Thought for the Day" program. The station gets dozens of requests each week for transcripts of the program. "People set their clocks by it," says Richard Weiss, senior editor at the *St. Louis Post-Dispatch* newspaper.

What's so unusual about this, you may ask? Richard Evans has been dead for over 26 years! He is kept alive in the minds and hearts of St. Louisians through audiotape. Morning news co-host Nancy Demko summed it up best when she said, "Being dead doesn't necessarily take you off the air here!"

Now that you understand the Popcorn & Picnics Values Group, don't stop now! Put your knowledge into action by completing the Exercises for Action on the next page.

EXERCISES FOR ACTION

Record your answers in your journal or notebook.

1. Think of a **personal** friend of yours who best fits the Popcorn & Picnics Group. In what ways will your enhanced understanding of this person help you interact with him/her better?

2. Think of a person you know through your **business** who best fits the Popcorn & Picnics Group. In what ways will your enhanced understanding of this person help you interact with him/her better?

3. Think of a time when you had difficulty interacting with a person from the Popcorn & Picnics Group. In what ways will your enhanced understanding of this person help you interact with him/her (and people like him/her) better in the future?

CHAPTER 11

Cars & Bars

Michael is in love with a young woman named LaShondra. She is the sexiest woman he has ever met. They are dating regularly, but things aren't going well. She always seems to be working or talking about work. LaShondra is a salesperson for the Acme Group and wants desperately to become the #1 producer, get noticed by the leaders of the company, and win that trip to Maui. She idolizes her boss and wants to be just like her. Michael feels left out. LaShondra seems to be more interested in making money and moving ahead at work than in their relationship.

Michael is driving himself nuts because he's dating a Cars & Bars woman, and he isn't a Cars & Bars man.

GROUP OVERVIEW

Cars & Bars are the Young and the Restless. Remember Michael J. Fox in the sitcom *Family Ties*? He was a stereotypical Cars & Bars. They are the "wannabes" who want to be successful and confident, but aren't. They have "bought into the system" by agreeing to work long and hard so that they can receive all the financial rewards that go with success. Because this group hasn't figured out the game yet and doesn't feel confident, they will use props to make themselves look successful. They will have a cell phone and pager even though they don't really need them. Even though they don't have a whole lot of money yet, they will "dress for success," go to all the "in" bars, and wear all the "in" clothes—all the while running up the balances on their six Visa cards. Cars & Bars are 17 to 38 years of age.

PRIMARY VALUE

Cars & Bars' Primary Value is *success*. In reality there are many ways to be successful in life, but to Cars & Bars it has to be *financial* success. They want to make tons of money!

◆

Cars & Bars' Primary Value is success.

◆

PRIMARY SPARKS

Their Primary Sparks are #1—Money, and #2—Inexpensive Status Symbols.

Primary Spark #1—Money

Cars & Bars crave money, but because they're young and just getting started, they don't have much yet. As a result, they will work long and hard on their jobs to move ahead to higher paying positions. Or they may be attracted to "get rich quick" opportunities like network marketing where there is the possibility of making a lot of money relatively quickly.

Primary Spark #2—Inexpensive Status Symbols

Cars & Bars want to *look* successful even though, in their minds, they aren't successful yet. So, when they're out on a date, they will order Beck's beer. When they see the boss at the office start to wear suspenders to work, they will go out and buy suspenders so they, too, can look like they've made it. When a new bar opens that attracts the "in crowd," they will stop going to their usual bar (something a Popcorn & Picnics would never do) and frequent the "in crowd" bar. They prefer to buy designer clothing, but usually they can only afford it on sale and pay for it with their ever-expanding list of credit cards.

PSYCHIC WOUND

Remember, a Psychic Wound is a pain that a particular Values Group will do almost anything to avoid. When you can "heal" someone's Psychic Wound and show them how to keep it healed, your relationship will be enhanced. When your product or service can heal people's Psychic Wounds, they will want to buy. Cars & Bars' Psychic Wound is *lack of confidence.* They *want* to be confident, but aren't yet. They desperately want to open the safe of success, but haven't cracked the code. When you can help a Cars & Bars friend be successful, your friendship will be enhanced. When you can show Cars & Bars how they can be more successful with your product or service, they will buy.

When you can "heal" someone's Psychic Wound and show them how to keep it healed, your relationship will be enhanced.

PREFERRED CARS

Remember, Cars & Bars want success. So what cars do they desire? BMWs, Mercedes-Benzes, Jaguars, and Porsches. Can they afford these cars if they're new? Not yet. So what kinds of cars do they buy? *Used* BMWs, Mercedes-Benzes, Jaguars, and Porsches on unique lease plans. These are the people with $600-a-month car lease payments and $300-a-month apartment rent! If they buy a new car, it will be a Camaro, Mazda Miata, or Mustang convertible. What colors do they prefer—brown, gray, or olive green? Heck no! They want orange, red, yellow, or black.

FAVORITE SOFT DRINK

Cars & Bars are young, hungry, and on the way up. They're the "New Generation!" And what does the new generation drink? Coke like all those old Popcorn & Picnics? Never! They want to "be young, have fun, drink Pepsi!" Pepsi commercials aren't anything like Coke commercials. A Pepsi commercial is not "a guy, his gal, their dog, and a truck" or a bunch of singing people on a hillside in Greece. Pepsi commercials are full of young, sexy people moving up in the world.

FAVORITE TELEVISION PROGRAMS

Cars & Bars are nuts for programs like *Baywatch*. All the Cars & Bars guys want a woman like Pamela Sue Anderson, and all the Cars & Bars gals want to look like Pamela Sue Anderson. MTV is their favorite cable channel. In 1997, *Singled Out* was their favorite program on MTV. *Singled Out* was a show where a sexy, young guy or gal picks a date from a group of 50 young, sexy people of the opposite sex by asking them a series of sexually loaded questions. One of the hosts used to be Jenny McCarthy, an ex–Playboy Playmate just bursting with hormones!

ADVERTISEMENTS DIRECTED TOWARD THEM

Remember the sexy print ads that got Calvin Klein into so much trouble—the ones with young models in various stages of undress? They were aimed directly at Cars & Bars. Another one is the Nissan animated TV commercial where the young male doll is recklessly driving his toy Nissan sports car through the house. He slides the convertible to a stop in front of a dollhouse, and beckons a "Barbie-ish" looking female dressed in a tennis outfit down for a ride. She comes down the elevator a second later, "dressed to kill" in a slinky, low-cut gold dress. As they drive away to the tune of *Girl, You Really Got Me Now,* the jilted, Ken-ish-looking former boyfriend looks down from the balcony in disbelief! At the end of the commercial, "Life is a journey. Enjoy the ride" flashes on the screen. Cars & Bars look at that commercial and shout, "I want a Nissan, now!"

PREFERRED CLOTHING AND CLOTHING STORES

Cars & Bars prefer sexy, bright, and tight clothing that reveals lots of skin. A Popcorn & Picnics guy will unbutton a maximum of one button on his shirt. A Cars & Bars guy will unbutton as many as the law allows. Cars & Bars females love short, low-cut, tight, "trashy," black dresses to wear to their favorite bars. Both male and female Cars & Bars wear clothing that shouts, "Look at me!"

Cars & Bars are the mall shoppers in stores like The Gap and The Limited. They will shop at more expensive stores like Nordstrom, but only during the twice-yearly sales. (Maybe not even then because their Nordstrom credit card is probably maxed out.)

TYPICAL BUMPER STICKER

"I PLAY COED NUDE VOLLEYBALL!"

FAVORITE BEERS

Michelob used to own this Values Group with their "The Night Belongs to Michelob" TV commercials. Those commercials always took place at night. (Guess what else takes place at night?) There were always lots of attractive young people having a great time at parties. Do you remember the one where three young guys were leaving a party through the door as three young and sexy young ladies walked by them on their way inside, and the three guys made a quick U-turn and followed them in?

Unfortunately for Michelob, Cars & Bars can be extremely fickle. They will drink Michelob for a year, then switch to Corona for a year, then switch to Coors Silver Bullet (the Cars & Bars' beer of choice as I write). What's in a Silver Bullet commercial? If it's summertime, there are young men and women frolicking on the beach in orange bikinis and tight Speedos. If it's wintertime, the young people are scrambling around the Rockies playing games. My favorite commercial is where two guys are playing Frisbee with their dog, and one of them throws the Frisbee over a mountain. The dog goes to get it, but doesn't come back. They go looking for Fido and find him with two attractive females who are petting him. The two guys look at the dog, look at each other and say, "Good boy!" The commercial ends with another sexy young lady slamming a beer spigot into a keg of Coors Light. (There may be a little bit of symbolism in her doing that with a big ol' smile on her face.)

HERE'S WHAT CARS & BARS ARE LIKELY TO WANT IN A RELATIONSHIP WITH YOU:

Husband/Wife Relationships

Cars & Bars want you to support them in being successful. They will usually help you, too. They want to go out with you to all the "happening" places. Because success and sex are at the top of their lists, they will want a robust sex life with you.

Parent/Child Relationships

If you are the parent of a Cars & Bars child, they also want you to support them in their success. When you can, it's important that you support them with their education and in learning the skills of success. Be careful of doing things like paying off their 12 maxed-out credit cards. There are some valuable lessons they must learn on their own. Also remember that this is a phase they're going through. Their definition of success will probably change as they mature.

Friendships

Again, the Cars & Bars will want you to support them in being successful. They may want you to attend networking meetings so you both can meet new people who will help you with your careers. Be careful of overspending in trying to keep up with your Cars & Bars friends.

Work Relationships

If you are the manager of a Cars & Bars person, you will have an eager, perhaps overly aggressive learner on your hands. They may want you to be their mentor. So teach them "the ropes" in your business. Support them in learning new skills that will help them get ahead in the organization. Show them how they can get to where they want to go by doing what you would like them to do.

If you are being managed by a Cars & Bars, help them get ahead in the organization by being a superb producer. If appropriate, sing their praises to their superiors.

If you are a work associate of a Cars & Bars, realize that they may seem overly aggressive in their quest to be successful. If it seems right, hook up with them and thrust ahead together.

Sales Relationships

Remember, when selling to any Values Group, ask yourself, "How can I provide them with their Values and heal their Psychic Wounds?" Cars & Bars' Primary Value is *success*. Show them how your product or service can make them more successful. If you're selling in a business-to-business situation, show them how buying from you will make them look good in the eyes of their superiors.

Cars & Bars' Psychic Wound is *lack of confidence*. Show them how your product or service will make them feel more confident or be a status symbol.

Remember, when selling to any Values Group, ask yourself, "How can I provide them with their Values and heal their Psychic Wounds?"

Service Relationships

Unlike the Popcorn & Picnics, Cars & Bars don't want a warm, fuzzy relationship with you. They want service that will make them look good and give them confidence. They want to be treated like they've made it, even though they haven't.

Cars & Bars are in a hurry. After they reach the age of 40, they start looking and acting goofy. It's easy to look at an over-the-hill Cars & Bars person and say to yourself, "It's time to grow up, Sparky." Most of them know this so they're in a hurry to "make it big" NOW!

How many Cars & Bars people popped into your head as you read this chapter? Take the next step now to enhance your relationships with them by completing the Exercises for Action on the next page!

EXERCISES FOR ACTION

Record your answers in your journal or notebook.

1. Think of a **personal** friend of yours who best fits the Cars & Bars Group. In what ways will your enhanced understanding of this person help you interact with him/her better?

2. Think of a person you know through your **business** who best fits the Cars & Bars Group. In what ways will your enhanced understanding of this person help you interact with him/her better?

3. Think of a time when you had a conflict with a person from the Cars & Bars Values Group. In what ways will your enhanced understanding of this person help you interact with him/her better in the future?

12

Polos
& Porsches

J im is a salesperson for International Widget. For the past eight months, he has been trying to sell his products to Elizabeth, the wealthy owner of a small but rapidly growing company. Even though Jim's widgets are the best value around, he can't seem to get to first base with Elizabeth. She will listen to his story, but quickly dismisses him saying, "Your product just isn't what I'm looking for!" In addition, Jim feels a little self-conscious around her, as "she dresses much better than I do." When Jim parks his Ford Taurus at her business, he sees her Infiniti Q45 parked in the choice parking space right next to the front door. Jim has just heard that she placed an order with a competitor who makes a similar widget to his at a significantly higher price. Jim is struggling with the account because he is a Popcorn & Picnics man selling to a Polos & Porsches woman.

GROUP OVERVIEW

The Cars & Bars Values Group *wants* to be successful. The Polos & Porsches Values Group *is* successful. The Cars & Bars Values Group *wants* to be confident. The Polos & Porsches Values Group *is* confident. The Cars & Bars Values Group *wants* lots of money. The Polos & Porsches Values Group *has* lots of money. The Cars & Bars Values Group hasn't cracked the code yet. The Polos & Porsches Values Group is already in the vault.

As you can see, Cars & Bars desperately want to be Polos & Porsches. In their eyes, the Polos & Porsches have made it. In some ways they're right. Polos & Porsches are usually making over $125,000 a year and may be at the top of their company, division, or sales group.

PRIMARY VALUE

The Polos & Porsches' Primary Value is to *uniquely be the best*. They want to be unique by having the best of everything—the best car, the best house in the best part of town, the best clothes, the best golf clubs stored at the best country club in the area.

---◆---

The Polos & Porsches' Primary Value is to uniquely be the best.

---◆---

PRIMARY SPARKS

Their Primary Sparks are #1—Winning the Game, and #2—Expensive Status Symbols.

Primary Spark #1—Winning the Game

Whether it's Donald Trump winning the real estate game, Bill Gates winning the information revolution game, Helen Gurley Brown winning the women's magazine game with *Cosmopolitan,* or Ted Turner winning the broadcasting game, Polos & Porsches are driven to be winners. In their minds, when you win the game, you're the best, and money is what they use to keep score.

Primary Spark #2—Expensive Status Symbols

Whether it's an obvious status symbol like a Porsche or a not-so-obvious status symbol like a Polo golf shirt, this group must show the world that they are uniquely the best. There is an interesting dynamic going on between the Cars & Bars Values Group and the Polos & Porsches Values Group. As you will recall, one of the Cars &

Bars' Primary Sparks was status symbols also. Well, the Cars & Bars decide which status symbols to buy by watching what the Polos & Porsches already have. This really upsets the Polos & Porsches because, in their words, "Only *we* should have these status symbols, not you wannabes."

Here's an example of this copycat dynamic in action. The Polos & Porsches were the first ones to buy Mont Blanc pens. They paid $160 for theirs because they bought them in exclusive stationery shops. The Cars & Bars saw those pens at work and said, "Ooooooooh, for $90 (they buy their Mont Blanc pens at Office Depot) I too can look like a Polos & Porsches!" The Polos & Porsches see the Cars & Bars' Mont Blanc pens and don't feel like they're the best anymore. So they give the Mont Blanc pen to their 17-year-old daughter and go out and buy a $450 Waterman pen. They feel they must stay one step ahead of those pesky Cars & Bars.

PSYCHIC WOUND

Polos & Porsches' Psychic Wound is *being one of the pack.* Popcorn & Picnics want to be one of the pack; Polos & Porsches hate it. In his "Competitive Edge" program, Anthony Robbins tells a revealing story about the Young & Rubicam advertising agency. They saw that the Merrill Lynch stockbrokers were running a series of commercials that showed a hundred bulls running across a dusty plain in Idaho. The commercial's tag line was, "Merrill Lynch is bullish on America." This commercial was aimed at the Polos & Porsches Values Group. What does this group think about a hundred stinky bulls whipping across some dusty plain in Idaho? They don't identify with that at all!

So Young & Rubicam said to Merrill Lynch, "Give us your multimillion dollar ad budget, and do you know what we'll give you? One studly bull. We'll even dye the bull for you so it looks more unique. And do you know where we're going to put him? In a china shop surrounded by hundreds of thousands of dollars of china and crystal. This upscale, dyed bull will carefully make the correct decisions to find the precise path through the china. And the tag line will be 'Merrill Lynch—a Breed Apart.'" Now that's a commercial the Polos & Porsches can relate to. Merrill Lynch's business went up considerably after the new ads started running.

The Lincoln Town Car ads of a few years ago did an extremely effective job of stirring up the Psychic Wound of Cadillac owners in America. At the time, General Motors was trying to save on development costs by making all their brands (even Cadillac) look similar. The ad featured a well-dressed Polos & Porsches couple coming out of a fancy restaurant. They ask the valet to bring them their Cadillac. The valet then pulls up in a Chevy. The woman looks at the guy in disgust as he tells the valet, "Go get my Cadillac!" The valet comes back a second time with a Pontiac. This makes the couple even more agitated and ashamed because now a crowd of fellow Polos & Porsches are looking at them. He asks the valet again, "Go get my Cadillac!"

In the meantime, another Polos & Porsches couple comes out of the restaurant. The obviously rich and confident man says to another valet, "My Lincoln Town Car, please." The valet has no trouble finding the right car. He immediately comes back with the Lincoln. The man slips the valet a $20 bill and the couple triumphantly drives away as the Cadillac couple looks on in horror.

The lesson is obvious and compelling. Show people how your product or service will heal their Psychic Wound, and they will want to do business with you.

PREFERRED CARS

By now I'll bet you're one step ahead of me. Did you think of Mercedes, BMW ("Extraordinary Cars for Exceptional People"), Infiniti, Jaguar, Lexus, and Porsche, Lincoln, or Cadillac? If you did, you are right! Their cars must be the best. They must be expensive. (Polos & Porsche's *want* to pay more.) They must be unique. At one time, Sam Walton was the richest man in America. He drove an old, beat-up pickup truck. "This doesn't fit the mold," you might say. Well, Sam felt even more unique than those "Eastern big shots" driving their tank-like Mercedes-Benzes.

FAVORITE SOFT DRINK

Think hard on this one. What "soft drink" could be thought of as the best and unique? San Pellegrino or some other exclusive bottled water.

FAVORITE TELEVISION PROGRAMS

This Values Group would rather watch *Frasier* than *Home Improvement*. They really like CNN with programming such as *Wall Street Week* and *Crossfire*. They may watch some golf tournaments, especially the Masters (i.e., the best golf tournament in the world). They are very selective with their TV watching because they are too busy watching their investments grow. Popcorn & Picnics have IRAs and 401Ks. Polos & Porsches have sizeable stock portfolios.

ADVERTISEMENTS DIRECTED TOWARD THEM

The theme of all Polos & Porsches ads is, "Our products or services are the best. Our products and services are unique. You've worked hard. You're the best. You're unique. You deserve them." The tastefully done DeBeers diamond ads are a perfect example. A handsome and distinguished Polos & Porsches man surprises his beautiful Polos & Porsches wife with a stunning diamond tennis bracelet, because it's the best way to "tell her you would marry her all over again." A Cars & Bars guy would tell his wife with a faux (faux sounds better than fake) diamond tennis bracelet. A Popcorn & Picnics guy would tell his wife with a trip to Pizza Hut!

Another great Polos & Porsches TV commercial is for the Buick Park Avenue. Here's how it goes. "You're working late again. You look out the window and see that your car is the last one in the parking lot again. You go down to your car and slip into its plush leather interior. As you pull away, a contented smile comes over your face because you know that you deserve and have the best."

PREFERRED CLOTHING AND CLOTHING STORES

Polos & Porsches have the best clothing made from the best fabric from the best stores like Brooks Brothers, Needless Markup (I mean Neiman Marcus), Saks Fifth Avenue, or any store on Rodeo Drive in Beverly Hills. They will even buy shoes at Nordstrom when they're not on sale. Designer clothing is preferred. Armani suits and Bruno Magli shoes are in their closets. They don't mind paying $180 for a Polo golf shirt with the little Polo guy on the chest when they could pay $32 for the same quality shirt in a store brand.

A Polos & Porsches wouldn't be caught dead in a Kmart. Popcorn & Picnics love to shop there. Cars & Bars don't like to be seen there, but will slip in just before closing to buy inexpensive toothpaste and paper towels. After all, they have a $600 car payment that's due!

TYPICAL BUMPER STICKER

None. Polos & Porsches don't want to mess up their new Lexus LS 400 with a "tacky" bumper sticker.

FAVORITE BEERS

If they do drink beer, Polos & Porsches want what they believe is the best beer—Heineken, Beck's, or, if they drink a light beer, Amstel Light. Because beer is perceived as such a common drink, they may prefer to drink an expensive single malt scotch.

HERE'S WHAT POLOS & PORSCHES ARE LIKELY TO WANT IN A RELATIONSHIP WITH YOU:

Husband/Wife Relationships

Balance is important in life, and sometimes Polos & Porsches can get out of balance with their drive to be the best and win the game. Spouses of people from this Values Group can help their mates win the game as they help them balance their lives. The spouses may also feel some pressure to be the best.

Parent/Child Relationships

It can be tough being the child of parents from the Polos & Porsches Values Group. They may have unrealistically high expectations, and want their children to be the best at everything they do. Taken to the extreme, this can create active and passive resistance on the children's part. If you're a Polos & Porsches parent, maybe you should back off a little and let your children develop in their unique ways at their unique speed. If you're the child, understand your parents' desire to want the best for you as you become your own person.

Friendships

Polos & Porsches are so busy winning the game they may not take much time for the few friends they do have. But because their friends are probably Polos & Porsches too, they understand.

Work Relationships

Because Polos & Porsches have made it, they are often in leadership roles in a business. If you work for Polos & Porsches, help them create the best company possible so they can win the game.

Sales Relationships

The story at the beginning of this chapter was about a Popcorn & Picnics trying to sell to a Polos & Porsches executive. Jim should have shown Elizabeth how his widgets were the best—something totally unique that will help her win the game. He also could have shown her how his widgets were so unique that they would heal her Psychic Wound of being one of the pack.

Service Relationships

Take a wild guess at what kind of service Polos & Porsches want. You guessed it—the best, service that is so wonderful and totally unique that they will feel that their hard work is being rewarded. The great part is that they are willing and able to pay for it!

Ritz-Carlton Hotels are renowned for their superb service. They have made the Diamond Touch a way of life for all their employees. Listen to this excerpt from the Ritz-Carlton Credo: "The Ritz-Carlton experience enlivens the senses, instills well-being, and fulfills even the unexpressed wishes and needs of our guests."

Aren't all these Values Groups interesting? Each group has its strengths and weaknesses—its idiosyncrasies and foibles. Understanding what makes each group unique and then acting on your understanding will make your life more interesting, enjoyable, and rewarding. Act now by completing the Exercises for Action on the next page.

EXERCISES FOR ACTION

Record your answers in your journal or notebook.

1. Think of a **personal** friend of yours who best fits the Polos & Porsches Group. In what ways will your enhanced understanding of this person help you interact with him/her better?

2. Think of a person you know through your **business** who best fits the Polos & Porsches Group. In what ways will your enhanced understanding of this person help you interact with him/her better?

3. Think of a time when you had a conflict with a person from a different Values Group. In what ways will your enhanced understanding of this person help you interact with him/her better in the future?

13

Degrees
& Dolphins

ose is an information processing specialist servicing large corporate accounts for his company, Infomania. His primary customer in the corporation, Melissa, never seems satisfied with his work. She is constantly requesting what seems like a ton of statistics, documentation, and reports. In fact, when Jose first started servicing the account, she had a lengthy interview with him to discuss his education and work experience. Jose knows he is doing an excellent job on the account, but all the paperwork and non-productive time spent with Melissa on the "other stuff" is driving him crazy. Instead of going nuts, Jose should realize that he is servicing a person from the Degrees & Dolphins Values Group. He should give her what she wants in the way she wants it, even though it doesn't seem "natural" to him.

GROUP OVERVIEW

Degrees & Dolphins is the fastest-growing Values Group. They are the people who want to make a difference in the world. They want to make the world a better place to live because, as they say, "We're all passengers on Spaceship Earth." They're environmentally oriented so they tend to belong to groups like the Sierra Club, Save the Whales, and Greenpeace. These people gladly recycled their garbage before they had to. They got very upset when spotted owls were being threatened by the logging industry in the Northwest. They went on strike against the tuna companies that were catching innocent dolphins in their nets.

Degrees & Dolphins are also very health conscious. They tend to eat healthy, natural foods and exercise regularly. They read *Prevention* and *Men's Health* magazines. They go to alternative health care providers such as chiropractors, herbalists, massage therapists, and acupuncturists. They may meditate and/or practice yoga. They support having cigarette smoking banned in all public places.

Degrees & Dolphins are flocking to the Pacific Northwest or the Silicon Valley so they can have a higher quality of life and work for intelligent companies like Microsoft or Intel. They're even intelligent about the number of children they have—not more than two, "world overpopulation, you know." Their two children even have intelligent names—Megan, age seven, and Nicholas, age two, for example. They have two children five years apart, unlike the Popcorn & Picnics who have five kids two years apart! When you go over to Megan and Nicholas's house, what do you see all over the place? Educational toys, that's what! Their house is one big learning laboratory. Megan and Nicholas already have their own computers and there's a telescope in Megan's room. Degrees & Dolphins have computers and telescopes. Popcorn & Picnics have sandboxes and tree houses. If married, Cars & Bars probably don't have kids yet; "Maybe some day, when we're more established."

PRIMARY VALUE

Degrees & Dolphins' Primary Value is *intelligence.* A large percentage of them have college degrees. Many have graduate degrees. This is the group most likely to belong to Mensa—the international society of geniuses.

PRIMARY SPARKS

Their Primary Sparks are #1—Formal and Informal Education, and #2—Action that Makes the World a Better Place to Live.

Primary Spark #1—Formal and Informal Education

Degrees & Dolphins believe that the best way to be intelligent is to receive formal education at a high-quality institution of learning. They often send their children to private schools because "You can't get a good education at public schools anymore." They also believe that you need to be a lifelong learner so they love going back to college even into their 40s, 50s, and 60s.

Degrees & Dolphins also learn informally. They read a lot of books. The books must be intelligently written fiction and non-fiction, "Not those trashy Danielle Steele so-called novels!" They attend numerous lectures and never miss seeing Dr. Wayne Dyer or Dr. Deepak Chopra when they come to town. They attend experiential weekend retreats to do things like getting in touch with their inner child.

Primary Spark #2— Action that Makes the World a Better Place to Live

From what you know about Degrees & Dolphins, do you think they would more likely be a Republican or a Democrat? Probably a Democrat. "After all, Bill Clinton and Hillary Rodham Clinton (Popcorns & Picnics still have trouble with 'that Rodham stuff') truly care about people. That mean old Bob Dole and that Grinch-like Newt Gingrich don't give a darn!"

They want to do business with companies that care about the environment, so they will shop at the Nature Company, the

Body Shop, funky little health food stores, and co-ops. The Degrees & Dolphins gladly volunteer their time and money to improve Spaceship Earth and make the world a better place for all of us fellow travelers.

PSYCHIC WOUND

Their Psychic Wound is *being manipulated by the system.* They don't trust big corporations because they have way too much power to manipulate government policy and people. When those huge and powerful companies Budweiser or Miller Brewing secretly buy their favorite microbrewed beer, they stop drinking the beer even though it's the same stuff. "It just doesn't taste as good now that Budweiser makes it!"

If you're a little (or a lot) skeptical of the information in this section, it probably means that you're a Degrees & Dolphins. You believe that this information can be used to manipulate people. In reality, you're right. The Values Groups information can be used in ways to trick people so that they lose and you win. As you will learn in Chapter 16, you will only want to use the Values Groups information to create win-win relationships.

I once did a Values Program in Portland (heavy-duty Degrees & Dolphins territory) where I discussed the Values Groups information. One woman in the group was a stereotypical Degrees & Dolphins. She got very upset because, in her words, "I don't want to be pigeonholed!"

PREFERRED CARS

If Degrees & Dolphins aren't making a whole lot of money, they will buy a Hyundai because you can get the most car for your dollar with Hyundai. If they're making a little more money, they will buy a Subaru because "Subarus are inexpensive and built to stay that way!" Also, with Subaru's line of four-wheel drive cars, you can go almost anywhere in the great outdoors. If they're making a little more money, they will buy a Honda Accord or a Toyota Camry. The Accord's advertising theme in 1997 and 1998 is "Simplify," which appeals to the Degrees & Dolphins who believe that life has gotten too complicated. If they're making even more money, they will buy a Volvo or a Saab—*intelligent* luxury, not extravagant luxury like Mercedes and Jaguar. As you can see, Degrees & Dolphins prefer buying foreign cars.

FAVORITE SOFT DRINK

What are some healthy soft drinks that Degrees & Dolphins prefer? Hansen's line of natural sodas or Snapple, "Made from the best stuff on earth." But what happened when the Degrees & Dolphins learned that the "big, mean" Quaker Oats Company bought their quirky Snapple brand? They stopped drinking the stuff! It's also interesting to note that Howard Stern, a Degrees & Dolphins favorite, jump-started Snapple with paid endorsements on his radio program.

Do you remember the scene from Steve Martin's movie, *L.A. Story,* where a group of people were sitting in a restaurant and each one of them was trying to outdo the other with their coffee order to the waitress? "I want a whipped, double Swiss mocha, decaf Frappuccino with a touch of imported cinnamon and a mint sprig on top." When Degrees & Dolphins go out for a snack, they order a whipped, double Swiss mocha, decaf Frappuccino with a touch of imported cinnamon and a mint sprig on top and a scone (that's a fancy-shmansy big, dried biscuit for all you non–Degrees & Dolphins). Popcorn & Picnics would never order a scone. They order a grape drink and a jelly-filled doughnut with multicolored sprinkles on top.

FAVORITE TELEVISION PROGRAMS

Degrees & Dolphins' four favorite cable channels are PBS, the Learning Channel, the Discovery Channel, and A&E. They get nauseous when they even flip past "unintelligent" programs like *COPS*, *America's Funniest Home Videos*, *The Jerry Springer Show*, and *Ricki Lake*. They get their news from Jim Lehrer on the PBS *NewsHour*. They watch *Nightline* with Ted Koppel or Charlie Rose on PBS, not David Letterman or Jay Leno. Many people in this group would rather "curl up with a good novel than watch all that trash on TV."

ADVERTISEMENTS DIRECTED TOWARD THEM

The ads directed toward this Values Group must be low key and have a minimum of hype. Remember, they don't want to be manipulated. Premium ice cream is not the healthiest stuff on the planet, but Degrees & Dolphins will feel good about eating Ben & Jerry's ice cream because it's made by a little nonconformist company in Vermont. One of Ben & Jerry's print ads shows you how you can order a poster of eight of the most famous social activists of our time. One of their most popular flavors is Cherry Garcia, named after Jerry Garcia of the Grateful Dead.

Would a hard-core Degrees & Dolphins rather use Procter & Gamble's Crest toothpaste or Tom's of Maine natural toothpaste? You guessed it! Degrees & Dolphins are so smart that they will spend $1.79 on a quart of Evian Water from the Alps. Why? "Because it comes from a glacier, so it must be healthy."

My favorite Degrees & Dolphins TV commercial is the Grape Nuts one where the guy is walking outdoors in his robe — no fancy house, no expensive china or silverware. As he is walking along a forest trail scooping the Grape Nuts out of the box with his hand, he sees a small bunny cross his path. He smiles gently as he lets nature's handiwork hop by. In the background you hear a gentle voice singing, "You know when you've got it good." We don't say that *we* think you've got it good because you would think that we're trying to manipulate you into buying our wonderful Grape Nuts. So we say, "You know when you've got it good" so you think you're making the decision! Incidentally, what would a Popcorn & Picnics guy from Texas do with the bunny? Shoot it and have a bunny burger and a brew for dinner that night!

PREFERRED CLOTHING AND CLOTHING STORES

Not surprisingly, Degrees & Dolphins want intelligently designed clothing in natural fibers such as 100% cotton and 100% wool. "None of that cheap polyester, Popcorn & Picnics stuff." The clothing is well made, but not flashy or sexy. Earth tones such as brown, tan, and green are the hues of choice.

Even at work, the men prefer not to wear suits and ties. To them it's more intelligent to wear loafers, argyle socks, a comfy pair of Dockers slacks, an open collar L.L. Bean plaid shirt, and a corduroy jacket with patches on the sleeves. For casual day, he will wear his trusty pair of Birkenstock sandals, a pair of relaxed-fit Levi's jeans, and a plain shirt from the Lands' End catalog. He tops his intelligent look off with a pair of 1968-ish metal framed glasses, and a mustache or beard.

Women also prefer the retro look—a comfy pair of brown loafers ("high heels are disgusting"), a long brown skirt or pants (no panty hose, of course), a tastefully dull sweater from L.L. Bean, a necklace with a big crystal on it, and an Annie Hall-ish hat to top it off. Of course, they will wear no or only a little makeup and a plain hairdo (maybe a braid with a stick in it). For casual, she will wear a tie-dyed dress and her Birkenstock sandals. As you've probably noticed, with all the Values Groups, I'm exaggerating a bit to make my point.

TYPICAL BUMPER STICKER

"PRACTICE RANDOM ACTS OF KINDNESS AND SENSELESS ACTS OF BEAUTY."

FAVORITE BEERS

Think for a second: what would be an intelligent beer? Maybe a beer that doesn't have alcohol in it, like Sharp's or O'Doul's. Degrees & Dolphins are also attracted to microbrewed beers like Samuel Adams. Have you ever listened to a Samuel Adams radio commercial? No loud music; no obnoxious announcer; just the plainspoken Jim Cook. This guy's voice is a cross between Mr. Rogers and Elmer Fudd—not a manly Bud voice. And what is Jim talking about? He's not talking about football or chasing young blonde women around the beach. He's talking about his teeny little brewery in Boston that makes beer the old fashioned way. He says, "My beer is handcrafted" (like the Budweiser people make it with their feet!). "I brew my beer slowly and carefully. It takes us months to do what the big, powerful brewers do in days. So the next time you want to be intelligent about your beer drinking" (that's a good one!) "think about our teeny little brewery that creates handcrafted beer from Boston." They even make it seem like it's made in an intelligent city. None of that dumb St. Louis or Milwaukee stuff. What he doesn't tell you is that most of their beer is brewed in Pittsburgh by a contract brewer!

HERE'S WHAT DEGREES & DOLPHINS ARE LIKELY TO WANT IN A RELATIONSHIP WITH YOU:

Husband/Wife Relationships

Degrees & Dolphins want an intelligent relationship with you. They want to learn and grow with you. They want to have a dialogue (a favorite Degrees & Dolphins word) with you about intelligent subjects. They want to read books and attend personal growth seminars with you.

Parent/Child Relationships

If you're the parent of a Degrees & Dolphins child and you're a Popcorn & Picnics, for example, you may be saying to yourself, "Where the heck did this kid come from?" On the sitcom *Frasier,* isn't that what Frasier's dad, Martin, is always saying about him? Degrees & Dolphins want to be supported in their quest for knowledge. If you're a parent to a Degrees & Dolphins, you may have the opportunity to pay for a lot of college.

Friendships

If you're in the same Values Group as your friend, you probably have some of the same Values and Sparks, and the relationship will have common ground. But variety is the spice of life, and hopefully you will have some friends from different Values Groups. If you're a non–Degrees & Dolphins with Degrees & Dolphins friends, support them in their scholarly ways. Buy them a book by Carl Sagan, Steven Hawking, or Deepak Chopra. They will cherish it forever.

Work Relationships

If you're the manager of Degrees & Dolphins employees, allow them to learn and grow. Support their continual education however and whenever you can. If your manager is a Degrees & Dolphins, you will want to be very precise and complete in your work. They will want comprehensive plans and reports from you.

Sales Relationships

In sales, always be thinking, "What do they want and how do they want it?" *What* Degrees & Dolphins want is to be intelligent, so show them how your product or service is the intelligent choice. *How* Degrees & Dolphins want it is to be educated and to make a difference in the world, so give them all the details and documentation they want. If possible, show them how your product or service is friendly to the environment. Remember not to push them into a decision. Degrees & Dolphins hate overbearing salespeople. Allow them to make the decision at their own pace, and say things like, "Only *you* will know if this is the right decision to make now."

Service Relationships

The short story at the beginning of this chapter is an example of what it's like servicing a Degrees & Dolphins person. Jose should know that Melissa wants to be intelligent. She wants him to provide her with all the statistics, documentation, and reports she desires. He needs to impress her with his qualifications and the advanced training programs he has taken.

If I make a spelling or grammar mistake in this book, a person from which Values Group is going to call me? You guessed it—a Degrees & Dolphins. They can't sleep at night if they read a sentence that uses a preposition to end a sentence with. (My editor, a Degrees & Dolphins, almost passed out when she read that last sentence!)

As we go through the five Values Groups, I hope you're learning the qualities of each group and how the groups relate to each other. You will learn more about this important area in Chapter 15. For now, though, keep applying the information in this chapter to your life by completing the Exercises for Action on the next page.

EXERCISES FOR ACTION

Record your answers in your journal or notebook.

1. Think of a **personal** friend of yours who best fits the Degrees & Dolphins Group. In what ways will your enhanced understanding of this person help you interact with him/her better?

2. Think of a person you know through your **business** who best fits the Degrees & Dolphins Group. In what ways will your enhanced understanding of this person help you interact with him/her better?

3. Think of a time when you had a conflict with a person from the Degrees & Dolphins Values Group. In what ways will your enhanced understanding of this person help you interact with him/her better in the future?

CHAPTER **14**

Red Dog
& Rodmans

on and Marie Osgood have a 20-year-old son, Jeff. Jeff is a good kid, but he just can't seem to find his path in life. Even though he had excellent grades, he dropped out of college after a year and a half. He's a computer wiz; he's been working with them since he was ten when his parents bought him his first Apple. Since he dropped out of college, he has lost two good jobs as a computer programmer at local companies. He says, "They don't give me enough freedom to let me do what I want." Jeff has moved back home. He and a couple of his buddies are starting their own software company in Don and Marie's garage.

Don and Marie don't know what to do. Jeff doesn't seem to have "bought into" the system like their neighbors' kids have. (They both graduated from college and have "real" jobs.) Jeff just seems to be too independent. He never gets dressed up, always wears that disgusting grunge clothing. Don and Marie are baffled because they have hatched that new breed of young person—a Red Dog & Rodman. The group gets its name from their favorite beer and favorite NBA basketball player, Dennis Rodman.

GROUP OVERVIEW

The Red Dog & Rodman Values Group hasn't bought into the system like the Cars & Bars did. It's not that they're bad kids. It's just that they can be difficult to get along with. Like the Cars & Bars, they were raised by the Baby Boomers, but they have decided to take a different path than their parents. They are stubbornly independent, extremely computer literate, and very entrepreneurial. Sometimes they're called slackers by those who don't understand them. "Generation X" is another name for the Red Dog & Rodmans.

PRIMARY VALUE

Red Dog & Rodmans' Primary Value is *independence*. In effect they say, "If you go this way, we'll go that way. If you wear your cap forwards, we'll wear ours backwards. If you like to snow ski, we'll snowboard. If you like to watch the summer Olympics with swimming, gymnastics, and track, we'll watch the X Games on ESPN with street luge, rock climbing, and skateboarding. If you eat your potato chips out of a bag, we'll eat ours out of a can. If you think body piercing is disgusting, we'll pierce our ears (three times), our nose, our belly buttons, and other body parts too numerous and disgusting to mention!"

Red Dog & Rodmans' Primary Value is *independence*.

PRIMARY SPARKS

Their Primary Sparks are #1—Going Their Own Way, and #2—Using the New Technologies.

Primary Spark #1—Going Their Own Way

Red Dog & Rodmans are 16 to 32 years of age. They are a relatively small group of Americans who are following in the footsteps of the Baby Boomers, the huge group of people born between 1946 and 1964. The Red Dog & Rodmans feel left out because to them it seems like everything has always been geared toward the

Baby Boomers. To compensate for the feeling of being left out, and because they see some real opportunities that the Boomers are missing, Red Dog & Rodmans want to blaze their own path through life just like their hero Dennis Rodman does.

This group is very entrepreneurial. They are fed up with what's being offered to them. Red Dog & Rodmans don't expect the government to take care of them. A study showed that more of them believe in UFOs than believe there will be money left in the Social Security fund when they retire.

Primary Spark #2—Using the New Technologies

The Red Dog & Rodman Values Group was the first generation raised with computers. They, more than any other group, see the awesome power of the new technologies. They see that the rapid change going on in the fields of communication and information processing levels the corporate playing field and creates tremendous opportunities for those who are smart, flexible, and quick. Red Dog & Rodmans have seen what Bill Gates has done at Microsoft. They've seen Michael Dell start a computer company from his dorm room at the University of Texas and go on to become the #3 PC manufacturer in the world. They've seen Marc Andreesen and James Clark become billionaires in a day when their company, Netscape, went public. Red Dog & Rodmans see using the new technologies as their path of independence.

PSYCHIC WOUND

Their Psychic Wound is *being left out again.* Have you ever known a family that had two daughters two years apart in age? When the older sister was a senior in high school, she got straight A's, was the captain of the basketball team, and was homecoming queen. When her younger sister was a senior, did she get straight A's? Was she the captain of the basketball team? Was she homecoming queen? Probably not. Her older sister was "a tough act to follow," and the younger sister chose a different path through life. It's the same thing with Red Dog & Rodmans. They have always had to follow the "great and wonderful" Baby Boomers. They feel left out and are "striking out their own," blazing a unique, non-Boomer path through life.

In addition to "being left out again," the Red Dog & Rodmans are a little (and in certain areas a lot) cynical of the system. "We're not going to pay off the huge national debt you Baby Boomers built up. You borrowed against our future so you could have more of your Baby Boomer toys. You did it. You pay for it! Not only that, we're not going to be able to support your Social Security. There are too many of you and not enough of us!" They're basically right.

PREFERRED CARS

Red Dog & Rodmans don't have a lot of money yet, and they're not really interested in flashy Cars & Bars-type cars anyway. So they will buy entry-level cars like Dodge Neon, Toyota Corolla, or Nissan Sentra. In some parts of the country, a South

Korean car named Kia is marketed to Red Dog & Rodmans. The tag line on their TV commercials is, "It's about time everyone had a well-made car!" "It's about time" is the perfect way to present your product to this cynical group.

In 1996, Volkswagen began marketing their cars to Red Dog & Rodmans. "If you lease a Jetta or Golf now for our incredibly low monthly lease rates that even you poor Red Dog & Rodmans can afford, we'll throw in a bike rack and mountain bike that you can proudly put on the top of your car to let the whole world know you're on a different path!"

The above cars are the ones they would like to drive, but, like Jeff in this chapter's opening story, many are just getting started and living at home. So they're forced to drive Mom's minivan or Dad's "clunky" Lincoln Continental. It's driving them nuts, but they have to do it!

FAVORITE SOFT DRINK

Coca-Cola has marketed their Sprite brand perfectly to the Red Dog & Rodmans. Sprite has become the #3 brand in the U.S. How did they do it? First of all Sprite knew that Red Dog & Rodmans drink large amounts of soft drinks. They also knew that Red Dog & Rodmans don't want to drink Coke "like Mom and Dad" or Pepsi "like those obnoxious Cars & Bars." Sprite gave their TV commercials a counterculture feel by showing groups of kids wearing grunge clothing just "hanging," listening to rap music, and drinking

Sprite. The tag line is, "Image is nothing. Thirst is everything. Obey your thirst." It's ironic that Sprite is spending millions of dollars creating a unique image for their product and their tag line begins with, "Image is nothing."

Another Red Dog & Rodman soft drink is Mountain Dew. The commercials are a hectic collection of skateboarding, bungee jumping, sky surfing, snowboarding, and Gen X'ers speaking a language that vaguely resembles English. After all, when you're having all this wild and crazy fun, you need to "Slam a Dew!" (Translation—drink a Mountain Dew.)

Another Red Dog & Rodman soft drink that has attained cult status is Jolt Cola. They do no conventional advertising that I've seen, but their tag line on the can is a classic—"All the sugar and twice the caffeine!" How's that for a unique path?

FAVORITE TELEVISION PROGRAMS

Any program that has the capital letter X in its name is aimed at the Generation X Red Dog & Rodmans—*The X-Files*, the *X Games,* and the *Winter X Games* on ESPN. They also like to watch programs on MTV like *Beavis and Butthead* (their idols). Another MTV program they loved to watch was *The Real World* ("not like the artificial world all you other people live in"), where a group of six non-actor Red Dog & Rodmans lived together in a house or an apartment for three months. Video cameras followed them everywhere as they did all their Red Dog & Rodman activities.

Red Dog & Rodman TV programs and commercials are often shot with a jerky camera technique, weird camera angles, and have printing that looks like it was typed by an old typewriter with a bad ribbon. Because Red Dog & Rodmans have an incredibly short attention span, their programs move at a rapid pace and have very short scenes.

Because they are so into computers, Red Dog & Rodmans may not spend much time watching TV. A high percentage of them are spending their evenings surfing the Internet.

ADVERTISEMENTS DIRECTED TOWARD THEM

Procter & Gamble's Pringles were originally marketed to Popcorn & Picnics. This is a tough group to break into because they like things to stay the same. Popcorn & Picnics will eat their Bar-B-Que Flavored Lays potato chips until they die of fat-clogged arteries. So Pringles said, "We've got a product that's different because it's made from powdered potatoes and comes in a can. What group demands that its products be different? Red Dog & Rodmans, that's who! We'll position our product as an alternative to those greasy, messy chips that come in bags. We'll show a bunch of Generation X kids hangin' around the street, bangin' on garbage can lids, havin' fun, and eatin' Pringles. And not just a few Pringles. We'll teach them that they have to Slam the Stack (translation—eat the whole can)."

Another Pringles commercial shows a Gen X boy sitting on a stuffed chair in his living room. He dreams of where he would rather be—out on the slopes having fun. The next scene shows him still in his chair shooting down the snow-covered slopes. He goes past a cute girl and gives her a wave. Now, he's about to hit a big tree, but he magically goes right through it. (Red Dog & Rodmans think they're going to live forever.) He finally crashes (Red Dog & Rodman commercials have a lot of crashes in them) with a big smile on his face at the bottom of the hill.

Another skateboarding-laden set of TV ads aimed at the Red Dog & Rodmans is the Taco Bell commercials. (Even the cash-deficient Gen X'ers can afford a 59¢ burrito.) The tag line for all the Taco Bell commercials is, "Nothing ordinary about it, Taco Bell!" Again, you can see the "We go our own, non-ordinary way through life" theme in these commercials.

PREFERRED CLOTHING AND CLOTHING STORES

Red Dog & Rodmans prefer grunge clothing—baggy tops and baggy pants, or baggy shorts that come down to mid-calf. They have moved their waistlines down to the middle of their butts so they can show lots of underwear. They refuse to wear Nikes like everyone else. They will wear hiking boots or other counter-culture shoes, like Doc Martens. It's a hard-and-fast Spark that colors and patterns cannot match and that no article of clothing can be tucked in.

The Red Dog & Rodmans prefer old, worn-out clothing that they buy at thrift stores, Goodwill, or Salvation Army stores. They also like to buy Rusty and Billabong clothing at surf shops. A few alternative-clothing manufactures such as No Fear are beginning to market to this group.

TYPICAL BUMPER STICKER

"THERE IS NO GRAVITY. THE EARTH SUCKS."

FAVORITE BEERS

One of their favorite beers is Red Dog. The imagery in their commercials is a perfect fit for this group: not a bunch of Budweiser frogs or lizards hanging around the swamp near their home bar, but one independent dog strutting through the streets. The dog sees a group of Budweiser dogs. He looks at them defiantly, sneers, and keeps right on walking. He is an independent dog of a different color that doesn't follow the pack. He's a Red Dog!

Another one of their favorite beers (if you can call the stuff that) is Zima. Zima is not a beer. It's a "malt beverage" that tastes like the swamp the Budweiser frogs swim in. Why would any group latch onto a product like this? "Because it's **OUR** malt beverage, that's why!"

HERE'S WHAT RED DOG & RODMANS ARE LIKELY TO WANT IN A RELATIONSHIP WITH YOU:

Husband/Wife Relationships

Because people in this group are so fiercely independent, this is the least likely group to be married. In fact, single Red Dog & Rodmans may prefer a group of boy/girlfriends than "being tied down to" one boy/girlfriend. If you're married to a Red Dog & Rodman, your mate is going to want a lot of space. You may want to establish a set of clear-cut boundaries for both of you.

Parent/Child Relationships

If you're the parent of a Red Dog & Rodman, remember, "This too shall pass." Love them, accept them, and watch in amazement as they turn into responsible, productive adults—just like you did after your hippie days.

Friendships

Like Cars & Bars, Red Dog & Rodmans tend to hang out together. If you're from another Values Group and have a Red Dog & Rodman friend, it may be upsetting that he/she wants friends other than you. That's the price you may have to pay for the friendship.

In the past year, I've seen two romantic relationships break up because the male Red Dog & Rodmans spent way too much time surfing the Web and way too little time with their girlfriends.

Work Relationships

In most environments it can be challenging working with Red Dog & Rodmans because they are so independent. In addition to giving them reasonable amounts of independence, provide them lots of training so they are constantly learning and growing.

Most importantly, tap into their entrepreneurial spirit and new technology know-how to improve your processes, products, and services. Red Dog & Rodmans are rule breakers. Take advantage of this by letting them work on or lead innovative projects— projects whose outcomes are to discover new ways of doing things that are radically different. If you don't, they may leave, start a company in their garage, combine their talents with a few of their buddies, and come back to haunt you.

Don't expect loyalty to your company in the same way you gave it when you started your first job. Red Dog & Rodmans prefer to think of themselves as independent contractors. They're not planning on being with your company for their entire career. On average, they change jobs every four years and careers every ten years! They want to learn and grow by working on neat projects. Give them that opportunity at your company and you will have an immensely valuable asset.

Sales Relationships

As in all sales relationships, you want to heal the pain (Psychic Wound) the person is having and give them the pleasure (their Values and Sparks) they desire. In the case of Red Dog & Rodmans, their Psychic Wound is *being left out again.* Make sure your products/services help them be part of their unique, counterculture group. Help the Red Dog & Rodmans be independent by showing them how your products/services will make them look and feel different so they can feel the Spark of Going Their Own Way. Think like Taco Bell with their "Nothing Ordinary about It" advertising campaign. This group loves the new technologies. In 1996, Mountain Dew sold 50,000 of their loyal drinkers, Dew Dudes, a pager plus six months free air time for only $29.99. Then, once a week, Mountain Dew paged the buyers with an 800 number the Dew Dudes could call to win discounts and prizes from 20 companies, such as Killer Loop sunglasses, Sony Music, Doritos, Universal Studios, *Spin* magazine, and K2 in-line skates. Mountain Dew collected some nice "promotional considerations" from these companies. They also used the system to ask the Dew Dudes their opinions on their product, its advertising, and future promotions.

Service Relationships

Whenever possible, use the new technologies to provide your service. Have as much information as you can on the Internet. Give them the independence they desire by showing them how to do their own service. Red Dog & Rodmans love the independence that comes with learning.

I hope you find the information in this chapter fascinating and valuable. I can guarantee you one thing: You will never look at another television commercial the same way after today!

There are three vital points that I want to make about the Values Groups information:

1. The Values Groups are only useful generalizations. There will be times when the information doesn't fit. Whenever possible, ask the person the specific Values and Sparks Questions you learned in Chapters 4 through 9.

2. People can be a combination of two or more groups. I grew up in Iowa, so I will probably always have a heavy dose of Popcorn & Picnics in me. At the same time, I'm doing well financially now, and I want to create the best company and the best corporate programs I can. So now I'm a combination Popcorn & Picnics and Polos & Porsches. This still doesn't decrease the usability of the information. For example, as a family we still go on lots of vacations together. We just go to more expensive places now.

The second richest man in America, Warren Buffet, is another example of a combination Popcorn & Picnics and

Polos & Porsches. He still lives in the same old house in Omaha that he did before he made his billions. He still goes to the same modest office in his same old American-made car as he always has. He still plays bridge with his buddies at night (on the Internet now).

Here are some other famous Values combinations:

- Oprah Winfrey—Popcorn & Picnics, Degrees & Dolphins, and Polos & Porsches. Three rolled into one; maybe that's why she's so universally popular.

- Hillary Clinton—Degrees & Dolphins and Polos & Porsches. Maybe that's why she gets involved in some questionable land deals. By the way, her husband is more totally Degrees & Dolphins.

- Michael Dell—Red Dog & Rodman and Polos & Porsches. He likes to buck the system, and he's building a $25 million house.

3. People can move from one Values Group to another through time. Here are some common examples:

- Cars & Bars to Polos & Porsches (The young go-getter finally makes it big!)

- Red Dog & Rodman to Degrees & Dolphins (The Generation X'er matures and decides to fit in with the rest of the world a little.)

- Popcorn & Picnics to combination Popcorn & Picnics and Polos & Porsches (The hardworking good ol' guy and gal are rewarded for their efforts.)

- Popcorn & Picnics to combination Popcorn & Picnics and Degrees & Dolphins (The Iowa farm girl goes to college and begins to take a wider world view, to the dismay of her parents who paid for college.)

- Degrees & Dolphins to combination Degrees & Dolphins and Polos & Porsches (The '60s hippie who now owns her own large business—Jane Fonda is an example.)

This change in Values as people mature is the main reason why you will want to check in with people in your closest relationships every once in a while, especially if you see them acting "strange"—a tip-off of a Values shift.

Wasn't the information you learned in the last six chapters fascinating? You can use these useful generalizations whenever you don't have time to ask the Values and Sparks Questions. Now, apply the information in this chapter to your life by completing the Exercises for Action on the next page.

EXERCISES FOR ACTION

Record your answers in your journal or notebook.

1. Think of a **personal** friend of yours who best fits the Red Dog & Rodman Group. In what ways will your enhanced understanding of this person help you interact with him/her better?

2. Think of a person you know through your **business** who best fits the Red Dog & Rodman Group. In what ways will your enhanced understanding of this person help you interact with him/her better?

3. Think of a time when you had a conflict with a person from a different Values Group. In what ways will your enhanced understanding of this person help you interact with him/her better in the future?

15

Five Values Groups in One Melting Pot

Think about it for a second. Where does most of the humor come from in TV sitcoms? Why does Frasier have so many run-ins with his dad, Roz, Daphne, and Niles? Why did Sam and Diane constantly fight and finally decide not to get married on *Cheers*? Why are Will and his cousin Carlton at odds on *The Fresh Prince of Bel-Air*? The people in the above sitcoms belong to different Values Groups. When different Values Groups get together there will be conflict because they are playing the same game with different sets of rules. This "clash of rules" is the basis of most comedy.

From your knowledge of the previous five chapters, name the Values Group to which each of the following sitcom characters belongs. The answers begin on the next page.

Frasier

Frasier

Niles

Martin, Roz, and Daphne

Cheers

Sam, Coach, Woody, Norm, and Cliff

Diane

Rebecca

The Fresh Prince of Bel-Air

Will

Carlton and Hillary

Uncle Phil and Aunt Vivian

The Simpsons

Homer and Bart

Lisa and Ned Flanders

Mr. Burns

ANSWERS

Frasier

Frasier—Degrees & Dolphins. He wants to help people. Wears a sport coat, green shirt, and muted earth-tone tie.

Niles—Polos & Porsches. Highly successful psychiatrist. Wears an expensive suit, white striped shirt, and power tie.

Martin, Roz, and Daphne — Popcorn & Picnics. They aren't pretentious like the above two. They drink beer and keep an old TV chair around forever.

Cheers

Sam, Coach, Woody, Norm, and Cliff—Popcorn & Picnics. The good old boys. They will be friends for life. Never read books.

Diane — Degrees & Dolphins. College educated. Always reading books.

Rebecca — Over-the-hill Cars & Bars. Always trying to make it into the big time. Thought she had it when she was going to marry zillionaire Robin. Ironically, she married a plumber in the last episode.

The Fresh Prince of Bel-Air

Will — Red Dog & Rodman. Wears grunge clothing and hat backwards. Has trouble with authority.

Carlton and Hillary — Cars & Bars. They have bought into the system, unlike that renegade Will. Preppy clothing.

Uncle Phil and Aunt Vivian — Polos & Porsches. He has made it as a successful lawyer living in Bel-Air. They want the very best for their children.

The Simpsons

Homer and Bart — Popcorn & Picnics. They watch too much TV, drink too much Duff Beer, and make disgusting body sounds.

Lisa and Ned Flanders — Degrees & Dolphins. They're interested in education and the arts. Both of them are too "goody-two-shoes" for Homer and Bart.

Mr. Burns — Polos & Porsches. Stereotypical, greedy nuclear power plant owner who doesn't care about people or the environment.

As these fictional characters humorously illustrate, variety is the spice of life. It would be unbelievably boring if we all had the same Value System. In addition, this variety is necessary to make beautiful music together. How would a symphony orchestra sound if all the members played the same instrument? Pretty one dimensional, right? It's the same in life. We need all different kinds of people, each playing their own instrument, each finding their special niche to create a society that has variety, balance, and depth.

Another illuminating metaphor is a river with three currents. The upper current is composed of the Cars & Bars Values Group and, farther downstream, the Polos & Porsches Values Group. The middle current is composed of the Popcorn & Picnics Values Group. This is the widest current and acts as a buffer between the two outer currents. The lower current is composed of the Red Dog & Rodman Values Group, and farther downstream, the Degrees & Dolphins Values Group. Each of the currents is distinct, but there is some overlap at the edges.

Each current is a necessary component of the river. The friction between the currents sometimes creates bends and whirlpools in the river. These bends give the river character and charm. The currents are constantly changing in speed and volume.

This causes the river to rise and fall in its ever-varying journey to the ocean. All the currents are necessary to the success of the river.

I hope you see that, exasperating as it is at times, all the Values Groups are necessary for any group, large or small, to enjoyably move towards its destination.

EXERCISES FOR ACTION

Record your answers in your journal or notebook.

1. In your **personal** life, identify a relationship between two other people that has significant conflict. Is part of the conflict due to two different Value Systems? What are the two Values Groups?

2. In your **business** life, identify a relationship between two other people that has significant conflict. Is part of the conflict due to two different Value Systems? What are the two Values Groups?

3. Identify a relationship in your life where you have a friend from another Values Group. What do the two of you do to make the relationship close in spite of your differences?

4. What challenges might occur in the following relationships?

   a. a Polos & Porsches boss and a Popcorn & Picnics employee

   b. two Popcorn & Picnics parents and their 18-year-old Red Dog & Rodman child

   c. a Degrees & Dolphins worker and a Cars & Bars co-worker

In the last two sections, you have learned how to accurately discover what people want and how they want it. Now, your job is easy—you can give it to them whenever and wherever possible.

Read on now—the people in all your relationships are waiting.

4

Give It to Them

In the last fifteen chapters, you've learned about the principle of the Diamond Touch, as well as the Values and Sparks of the people in your most important relationships. This knowledge, however, is not power. Knowledge is only *potential* power. Knowledge put into **action** is power. In the next three chapters, you will put your knowledge into action by *intelligently* giving people what they want in the way they want it.

In Chapter 16, you will learn the art of Creative Giving—giving in ways that create a better life for the other person. In Chapter 17, you will learn how to create Value Links when you're in an influence relationship. Value Links are *the connections between your product, service, or idea and what the other person truly desires.* In Chapter 18, you will learn why everyone wins when you give creatively.

16

Creative Giving

As you've been reading this book, I'll bet you've asked yourself once or twice, *Do I have to give people everything they want right away?* The answer is a resounding no! If your daughter's highest Value in life is success and her Spark for success is having $1 million in the bank, you don't need to give her $1 million. You might not be able to pull together that much money, and it wouldn't be in her best long-term interest. You need to be creative with your giving. Educate her on the value of taking personal responsibility. Then help her learn how to earn and save the money on her own.

Let's start with the Foundational Rule of Giving: *Give to others in ways that create a better long-term life for them. Give to others in ways that are in their best long-term interest.* The exact method of giving will vary depending on the nature of the relationship and the goals of the people in the relationship.

------------◆------------

The Foundational Rule of Giving: *Give to others in ways that create a better long-term life for them. Give to others in ways that are in their best long-term interest.*

------------◆------------

After you discover someone's Values and Sparks, you have four options:

A. Give with no education or negotiation. In most relationships, this is the option that will occur most frequently. The gift is in the person's best long-term interest, and you can give it easily and gladly. For example, if your son likes to get out the baseball gloves and play catch with you, you can give him that gift on a regular basis with no education or negotiation. You get to spend some quality time together and he improves a skill that will help his contribution to his Little League team.

B. Educate, then give. This option depends on the nature of your relationship with the person. In your opinion, this person may need some education before the gift. This is especially true in parent/child relationships, some work relationships, and sometimes in influence relationships. You may have some knowledge they need to make a wiser choice concerning the best Sparks for their Values. For example, you're a manager at work, and one of your employees wants to be assigned to a certain project team. You may have to educate that person by helping him or her acquire the skills needed to join the team. You help the employee enroll in a class to learn the skills, and then you assign him or her to the project team.

C. Negotiate, then give. In all six kinds of relationships covered in Section 2, you may need to negotiate "the rules of the game": that is, you may need to negotiate on the Sparks you can (or want to) give. Be sure to ask the question, "How can we create a win-win situation here?" For example, if your son wants to extend his curfew on weekends from 10 P.M. to midnight, you can negotiate an 11 P.M. curfew. When it comes to negotiation, it's important to remember that both parties can be winners. A great way to accomplish this is to ask a question using the word *and* to connect the wins. For example, in Chapter 4, a wife asked her husband, "What can I do when I don't like something you've done so I can get my point across *and* you feel respected?" The husband answered, "You can say you don't like what I just did without making me seem like I was wrong. You can ask me not to do something instead of demanding that I don't do it." The husband and wife both win in this negotiation.

D. **Don't give.** This is your option of choice if you *can't* give it to them, or *don't want* to give it to them because you don't feel it's in their best long-term interest. Be sure to explain to the person why you don't want to do it. For example, a friend is requesting that you help him pull off a shady business deal. You can say, "No way!" and then explain why.

If you **do** give, as in A, B, or C, you can do any of the following:

1. **Give them all of what they want, in the way they want it.** This choice usually goes with option A. The playing catch with your son example falls into this category.

2. **Give them some of what they want, in the way they want it.** This choice usually goes with options B and C. Your reason for not giving them all of what they want should be made clear in the education or negotiation process. The example of curfew negotiation falls into this category.

3. **Support or clear the path for their getting what they want, in the way they want it.** You may not be the person who actually provides the Sparks for the achievement of their Values. You may elect to support them on their journey to their Values or clear the path to make the journey quicker and safer. The person who wanted to be on the project team example falls into this category.

If you **don't** give it to them (option D), explain why you can't or don't want to and then do any of the following:

4. **Accept your differences in Values and/or Sparks.** Agree to disagree. Most relationships aren't a perfect match of Values and Sparks. You may want to accept any differences in the rules of the game that can't be resolved. At least you know where the differences lie, which can be very helpful. For example, if your son asks for a midnight curfew, and you believe that this isn't appropriate at his age, you don't have to give it to him or negotiate. Explain why you're making the decision to leave his curfew at 10 P.M. Tell him you love and respect him, and agree to disagree.

5. **End the relationship.** If appropriate, refer them to someone who may give them what they want in the way they want it. This is the last resort and will not

happen very often if you practice the Diamond Touch with skill and caring. For example, if a prospect of yours asks for something that you can't deliver, and all your education and negotiation efforts aren't effective, refer the person to someone who may be able to help.

If you **do** give it to them with 1, 2, or 3, you can make any of these choices:

a. **Give now and regularly in the future.** If possible and appropriate, provide the Spark so they can feel the emotion and the desire right now! Then give it to them on a regular basis in the future. For example, tell your wife you love her in that certain tone of voice with that "special" embrace right now and every day from now on if that's her Spark for love.

b. **Give now and variably in the future.** If possible and appropriate, provide the Spark so they can feel the emotion and the desire right now! Then give it to them on a variable basis in the future. Maybe something has to happen first in order for it to be appropriate for you to provide the Spark. Unexpected surprises also have great power. Winning a slot machine jackpot is thrilling because you don't know it's coming. You may choose to provide a Spark at unexpected times to create a special moment. For example, every once in a while, surprise your spouse with flowers.

c. **Give later and regularly in the future.** You may not be able to provide the Spark immediately. Do it as soon as possible and regularly in the future. For example, you discover a client you're servicing wants telephone conferences with you once a week. If it isn't possible this week, give it to them starting next Tuesday and every Tuesday thereafter.

d. **Give later and variably in the future.** You may not be able to provide the Spark immediately. Do it as soon as possible and variably in the future for the same reasons as outlined in b. For example, you discover that a friend likes written notes from you. Write the person a note next week and every once in a while from now on.

On the preceding pages, I've given you many possibilities for giving. The Giving Process Flow Chart on the next page will tie everything together.

THE GIVING PROCESS FLOW CHART

Discover Their Values and Sparks

then   **or**

A. Give with no education or negotiation.   D. Don't give.

B. Educate, then give.

C. Negotiate, then give.

and   **or**

1. Give all of it to them.   4. Accept your dfferences.

2. Give some of it to them.   5. End the relationship.
                                                Refer, if appropriate.
3. Support or clear the path for them.

and

a. Give now and regularly in the future.

b. Give now and variably in the future.

c. Give later and regularly in the future.

d. Give later and variably in the future.

Below are some examples of possible ways of giving. You may want to follow along with the Giving Process Flow Chart. All of the examples are taken from the dialogues in Chapters 4 through 9.

In Chapter 4, a wife discovered that her husband's Relationship Value was respect and his Spark was being hugged and told how proud she was of him. She can now provide the Spark with no education or negotiation. She can do that totally. She can do that now and regularly in the future. This will make him feel loved on a continual basis and probably increase the amount of love he returns to her.

Here's an example from Chapter 5. My daughter, Belinda, has a Value of fun for our relationship. One of her Sparks is playing computer games with me. I can easily provide that Spark with no education or negotiation. I can do that completely. And I can do that now and once or twice a week at unexpected times in the future.

Here's an example from Chapter 7. I discover that a work associate has success for a Job Value. The Spark for success is earning $30,000 a year. I can give it to him by providing vital learning experiences so he can gain the skills necessary to earn $30,000 a year. I can do that by having a meeting with him next Monday to develop our plan and then meet regularly in the future.

Your second option after you discover people's Values and Sparks is to educate and then give it to them. Here's an example from Chapter 5 on pages 54–58. As you will recall, Belinda said that self-esteem was one of her Life Values and that education was one of her Sparks. After I discovered that, we had an educating discussion about all the ways she could learn in life. Now I can support her education in the future by regularly helping her with her homework, providing a tutor when needed, and taking her interesting places.

I also felt some education was in order when she said that being popular was another of her Life Values, and "when everyone likes me" was her Spark. Go back to page 57 now and read this section. You will see that I tied in "saying no to drugs" with self-esteem and being successful in life (her top two Life Values). You will have tremendous educational impact anytime you show someone that an undesired behavior goes against their stated Values, or that a desired behavior will give them their stated Values.

I also described the education option in Chapter 9, page 112 when Chloe, the service provider, educated her customer, Bill.

Your third option after you discover people's Values and Sparks is to negotiate and then give it to them. Here's an example from Chapter 6 on pages 66–67. In this example, you broke your friend Tanya's Value of trust. You then negotiated the way you will regularly keep her trust in the future.

The negotiation option also appeared in Chapter 7, on pages 81–82 with Nate and Brad in a work situation. We negotiated a way that I could get the information I needed *and* Brad could receive the respect he desired.

Which way of giving is the best choice? The answer can be determined by these four questions:

1. What is the right thing to do morally, legally, and ethically?

2. What way of giving is in the person's best long-term interest?

3. Which way of giving will create the best life for the person?

4. Which way of giving supports my goals, dreams, and way of life? Consider your capacity for giving. If you over-give to too many people, you may lose in the long run because it will decrease your ability to give in the future when it's truly needed.

Remember, you won't always be perfect in your giving. Give, evaluate the results, and modify your giving. Effective giving is an art that takes experience to master. Now, you can continue your mastery of the Diamond Touch by completing the Exercises for Action on the next page.

EXERCISES FOR ACTION

Record your answers in your journal or notebook.

1. If you're married, discover your mate's Values and Sparks and then create a plan for giving it to him/her using the information in this chapter.

2. If you're in a parent/child relationship, discover the person's Values and Sparks and then create a plan for giving it to him/her using the information in this chapter.

3. In one of your friendships, discover the person's Values and Sparks and then create a plan for giving it to him/her using the information in this chapter.

4. In one of your work relationships, discover the person's Values and Sparks and then create a plan for giving it to him/her using the information in this chapter.

5. In an influence relationship, discover the person's Values and Sparks and then create a plan for giving it to him/her using the information in this chapter.

6. If you're in a service relationship, discover the person's Values and Sparks and then create a plan for giving it to him/her using the information in this chapter.

17

Elegant Influence

This chapter is about **elegantly** influencing people to take action. It's not just for salespeople. If you have children, you're in sales. If you want to get your ideas across at work, you're in sales. Elegant Influence is not about pushing people into a sale so that you win and they lose. Elegant Influence is the enjoyable process of getting people to want to take action for their reasons so that you *both* win.

In the last chapter, you learned that you have tremendous educational impact anytime you show someone that an undesired behavior goes against their stated Values, or that a desired behavior will give them their stated Values. (Remember my conversation with Belinda about drugs?) This idea is the core of Elegant Influence. It's an important part of the Pain/ Pleasure Principle. The Pain/Pleasure Principle says, "People take action out of their need to avoid pain and/or their desire to gain pleasure." See the diagram below.

PAIN ➡ ACTION ➡ PLEASURE

Let me give you an example of what I'm talking about. Why are you taking the time and energy to read this book? You're doing it because there is some pain in one or more of your relationships and you think that this book will help (avoid the pain) and/or you believe that this book will help you get more pleasure out of one or more of your relationships (gain the pleasure).

---◆---

Elegant Influence is the enjoyable process of getting people to want to take action for their reasons so that you *both* win.

---◆---

Here's another example. I do about 100 corporate and association presentations each year. People will come up to me at the events and ask, "How can you stand to do this? I hate public speaking!" They're not alone. Public speaking is the #1 fear in the United States today. Death is #2!

I love public speaking because I have **learned** that public speaking leads to pleasure. Yes, I do get paid for my presentations; however, I would do it in one form or another even if I didn't get paid. (Don't tell my clients this!) But it wasn't always this way. My first paid presentation was to Mutual of Omaha. It was a four-hour program for a group of their agents. After two hours, we took a 15-minute break. The head guy came up to me and said, "Nate, you're boring my people to death. Some of them are threatening to leave. I know you're supposed to do another two hours. Cut it short. Just do 15 more minutes!" Let me tell you, that was painful!

My second paid presentation was to IBM. (I like starting with the little guys.) Five minutes before I was to begin, I went to the restroom. To make a long story short, I couldn't get my zipper up! When I get under pressure, I sweat like crazy. So I went over to the sink to throw some cold water on my face. In addition, I had just purchased a new, burgundy tie so I could fit in with the IBM people. I leaned over the sink and created a two-tone burgundy tie with a huge water mark on the bottom. So I walked into the meeting room sweating like a marathon runner in a two-tone burgundy tie. To make things even more interesting the title of my presentation was

"Stress Management." This was a second painful experience with public speaking.

You might be thinking to yourself right now, "Nate, this story doesn't fit your Pain/Pleasure Principle. You got pain with your first two public speaking actions. You should have gotten the message and quit trying!" That's true, but there was another force at play in the equation. One empowering belief my parents taught me as a child was never to give up on your dream. "You have big dreams, Nate," they'd say. "Life is going to put roadblocks in your path to test you to see if you want your dreams badly enough. Most people give up when they hit the roadblocks. That's why they never reach their dreams. You're different. When you hit the roadblocks, you're going to see them as a sign that you're making progress. You're going to keep going so that you can have all the pleasure of living your dream!"

I'm a public speaker today because the pain of my first two presentations was less than the pain of giving up. My parents were elegant influencers. They used the Pain/Pleasure Principle to influence me to create my dreams in life.

You can do the same in your relationships. Discover the other person's Values and Sparks. Then show them how they can get the pleasure they desire in the way they want it by doing what you want them to do! The last sentence raises an interesting question. Isn't this manipulation? The answer is, "Yes!" When you get right down to it, all forms of influence are manipulative. You're influencing people to take an action they wouldn't do if you didn't interact with them.

Manipulation has gotten a bad rap. It isn't always bad. If your child comes home with a great report card, would you praise her? Sure you would. Would that be manipulation? Sure it is. It increases her chances of getting another great report card so she could again receive praise from a person she loves and respects.

Here's another example. As a society, do we expect our teachers to instill values such as honesty, respect, and fairness to their students? Of course we do. And how do they teach and reinforce these principles? Elegantly, with pain and pleasure. They are positively manipulating the children to teach them life skills that will benefit them and society. The key word in the last sentence was "positively."

With positive manipulation, the other person and you win. With negative manipulation, the other person loses and you win. Whether you consciously know it or not, you're manipulating all day long. The questions are:

1. Are you manipulating in ways that create wins for everyone involved?

2. How good are you at positive manipulation?

I trust that you will use the information in this chapter to create more wins for the people in your world. A hammer can be used to build or tear down a cathedral. Please use this information to build numerous cathedral-like relationships in your life.

Elegant Influence, then, is discovering people's Values and Sparks, then showing them how they can achieve those unique

Values and Sparks with the product, idea, service, or action you're "selling." In essence, you're creating a linkage in their brains. I call these linkages Value Links. See the diagram below.

Value Links are mental connections that show people how they can get what they want (their Values) in the way they want it (their Sparks). This connection will create desire. They will act on that desire with the acceptance of the product/idea/service/action that you propose. From now on, I will call your product/idea/service/action your PISA.

◆

Value Links are mental connections that show people how they can get what they want (their Values) in the way they want it (their Sparks).

◆

There are six powerful Value Links that you can use. I will discuss them one at a time and give you examples of each.

THE SIX VALUE LINKS

1. **Test Drives** — With a test drive, you have the person actually use your PISA. When you go to a car dealership and show even the slightest interest in a particular car, what does the salesperson do? She gets you into the car for a test drive. Have you ever taken a puppy or a kitten home for the weekend to see if the family will like it? Did you bring the puppy or kitten back? Probably not. You were on a test drive. Just yesterday, I had a copier salesperson in to tell me about his products. He discovered the copier I liked best and offered to bring it to our office to use for 30 days free of charge. That's a test drive.

   Test drives may be the most powerful form of Value Link because they get people using your PISA. This involves more than one of the five senses. They see, hear, feel, smell, or taste your PISA.

2. **Demonstrations** — With a demonstration, you **show** the person how your PISA works. In one of my corporate programs, I teach the participants how to break a wooden board karate-style. They don't **have to** do it. I want to elegantly influence them to **want to** do it. How do I accomplish this? I break a board first. Then I select someone from the group who I believe will be able to do it. I pick someone who isn't big and muscular, but

someone smaller and who has lots of energy. This person invariably breaks the board, which is an impactful **demonstration** for the others in the group. This greatly increases the number of people who then accept the challenge.

I teach dentists to elegantly influence their patients to accept treatment plans by using computer technology to show patients what their smile will look like after their cosmetic dentistry has been done. This visual demonstration increases case acceptance.

3. **Stories**—Great salespeople are great storytellers. This isn't a coincidence. People enjoy stories. They allow themselves to become the subjects of the stories. When this happens, they experience the same emotions and learn the same lessons as the story subjects. Let's say you want to influence your daughter to have more perseverance. You could preach at her, or you could tell her Michael Jordan's story. Michael always wanted to be a basketball player, but he was so uncoordinated as a teenager that he couldn't even make the tenth-grade basketball team. He didn't give up. He kept on working and became the greatest basketball player of all time. Which is more effective, the preaching or telling a story? You know the answer to that one.

In my corporate and association programs, I always back up my key points with stories. When I talk about being smart, flexible, and quick in our rapidly changing world, I tell a story about the *Encyclopedia Britannica* and a story about Michael Dell. The *Encyclopedia Britannica* had record profits in 1993. Do you know their financial status in 1995? Bankrupt! How can a company with a brand name like *Encyclopedia Britannica* end up in bankruptcy? They weren't smart, flexible, and quick about changing technology and went down the tubes in two years.

Michael Dell is smart, flexible, and quick. He started his company, Dell Computers, in his dorm room at the University of Texas. One day, he built his own, higher quality, lower cost computer. He had a few friends who asked, "Hey, can you build me a computer, too?" He built great computers for them. His friends had more friends who asked the same question. Now Dell is the #3 computer maker in the world. How can a kid pass up companies that have so many resources? He was smart, flexible, and quick.

When you want to elegantly influence someone, think, *What engaging story can I tell to get my point across?* Often, the most powerful stories are personal. You can also collect other people's stories to use at the appropriate times.

4. **Questions** — How many questions have I used in this book? Ooops, I just used another one didn't I?

Questions are such effective Value Links because they precisely direct the listener's mental focus. If I asked you the question, "What are you happiest about in your life?" your mental focus is directed to the things that make you happy. When this happens, you will feel happy.

Here are some examples of Value Link Questions. As you will see, the question can be preceded by statements that "set up" the question. Remember, the question is the Value Link. The two items being linked are bolded:

a. "Mr. Prospect, if you could receive those **savings** we talked about, would you be interested in trying out **our machine** for 30 days?" When he answers, "Yes," the link is formed.

b. "Ms. Dental Patient, in order for you to have the **smile** you've always dreamed of, you need to proceed with **Plan A or Plan B.** Which one looks best to you?" When the patient answers, "Plan B," the link is welded.

c. "Belinda, you've said that **self-esteem and success** are really important in your life. Do you see how **not taking drugs** will help you have more self-esteem and success?" When she answers, "Yes," the win-win link is made.

d. "Mary, you've mentioned that **success** is very important in your life and **making $50,000** a year is one of your Sparks for success. I hope you see that **coming to work for our company** will enable you to learn the vital skills you will need to command that salary in the near future. We would love you to start on the first of the month. How does that sound to you?" When she answers, "Yes," the link is completed.

A specific type of Value Link Question is called a Future Pace Question. With a Future Pace Question, you ask people how they're going to use your PISA in the future. For example, you're a real estate professional and you ask a family who shows interest in a particular house, "Which one of the kids would have this room for their bedroom?" That question directs their thinking into the future actually using the house as their own. After they answered the question, a strong Value Link is welded.

It's important to remember that Value Link Questions can influence the person to take a step in the "right" direction. It's usually better to have the person take several small steps on the way to the decision than one giant step at the end of the influence process. A Value Link Question can also be the final question asking the person to make the decision to "buy" your PISA.

5. **Metaphors** — Metaphors are an extremely useful form of Value Link when the concept you're explaining is a difficult one. Here are three examples:

   a. "Mr. Sanchez, the crown I recommend for that tooth fits over your tooth just like a thimble fits over your finger."

   b. "When implemented, Service Plan A will provide you with a money machine that will print you a $20 bill every 90 minutes."

   c. "Coming to work for our company will be like playing on that winning high school basketball team you mentioned. You will work hard, be challenged, and feel the thrill of victory on a regular basis!"

   As you can see, when you use a metaphor, you say, "**This** (the PISA I want you to understand) is like **that** (a concept you already understand).

6. **Feature/Benefit Statements** — A feature is a unique quality of your PISA. An office copy machine could have the following features:

   a. a speed of 20 copies per minute

   b. automatic document feeding

   c. simultaneous printing on the front and back of the paper

d. 20-sheet collating

e. automatic stapling

f. a single lease payment covering the machine and maintenance

A benefit is what the feature does for the user. Benefits are unique advantages that in some way make the buyer's company or life better. Benefits are ultimately determined by the buyer. As an Elegant Influencer, you can suggest benefits.

Some possible benefits (in the words of the buyer of the copier) features listed above are:

a. "We can **be more successful by saving time.** Now, we can do most of our printing in-house, which means no more 15-minute trips to and from the printer. All five features will allow us to print four times faster than the old machine we have now."

b. "We can **be more successful by saving money.** No more travel expenses. No more paying someone to drive to the printer. No more bills from the printer complete with sales tax. No more repair bills on our old machine."

c. "We can have **greater convenience.** We can just load the machine, push three buttons, and the machine will do the rest."

When it comes to influence, always remember this: **A feature is not a benefit unless it gives buyers what they want (their Values), in the way they want it (their Sparks).** Feature/Benefit Statements are the Value Links between your PISA's features and the buyers' Values and Sparks.

A Feature/Benefit Statement takes the following form. State or review your PISA's appropriate features. Then begin your next sentence with something like, "What this means to you is . . . " or "This will enable you to . . . " As an example, if you discovered with your Values and Sparks Discovery Questions that your customer wants to be more successful in her business, and saving time and money would help her do that, say the following Feature/Benefit Statement: "Ms. Hong, our Copy Master 3000 has a speed of 20 copies per minute, an automatic document feeder, simultaneous printing on the front and back of the paper, a 20-sheet collator, and automatic stapling. **What this means to you** is that you will be able to do all your copying in-house. Not only will you save time and money, it will be a lot more convenient for you. In addition, with our all-inclusive lease plan, you won't be paying those high repair bills you've been stuck with lately. **This will enable you** to operate more successfully by reducing your monthly expenses."

In review, you have six types of Value Links you can use to connect your PISA to people's Values and Sparks:

1. Test Drives

2. Demonstrations

3. Stories

4. Questions

5. Metaphors

6. Feature/Benefit Statements

When I teach influence programs to groups of salespeople, I help them create a toolbox full of the six types of Value Links. Then, they can pull the most effective Value Link out of the toolbox at the right time to create an ironclad link between their PISAs and the desires of their customers. When you learn to do this, influence becomes an art where you paint a different picture on the series of unique canvasses you face every day.

If you've been in an influence position for any length of time, you've probably had an occasion where you told the other person too much and lost the sale. What happened in that situation? You told the person about a feature of your PISA that didn't match their Values and Sparks. *You were prescribing without diagnosing.* They probably said something to the effect of, "I don't want that," or "You mean I have to pay for that!"

I consistently see influencers make two mistakes:

1. They try to influence everyone in the same way. They take the "spray and pray" approach to influence. This is like taking a garden hose and setting the nozzle on spray. You will cover a lot of ground, but you won't have much impact in any one area. When you discover exactly what your customer wants and how they want it, you can use the right Value Links to point a concentrated stream of your PISA's features at your customer. Now you will have impact!

2. They try to influence people through their own set of Values and Sparks. They think, "What's important to me will be important to them." This is usually a costly assumption. Going back to our garden hose metaphor, these influencers point a concentrated stream of water in the wrong direction and leave the customer's garden dry.

So far in this chapter, we've been talking about words. Words alone do have power, but maybe not as much as you think. You have three tools of influence at your disposal: words, voice qualities (**how** you're saying what you're saying), and body language. One research study showed that your words carry 7% of the influence power; your voice qualities 38%; and your body language 55%!

In addition to helping salespeople create a toolbox full of Value Links, I will often videotape them so they can see themselves in action. Most people are excited to see huge improvements in their effectiveness by enhancing their voice qualities and body language.

John F. Kennedy and Ronald Reagan were both extremely popular presidents. They were miles apart in terms of political philosophy, but they both had one trait in common. They were Elegant Influencers. They knew how to use their voice qualities and body language to effectively convey their messages.

When John F. Kennedy debated Richard Nixon, most experts who listened on the radio thought Nixon won the debate. Most experts who watched the debate on television thought Kennedy won the debate. Kennedy was far superior to Nixon when it came to the effective use of body language—a qualitiy that could not be transmitted by radio. TV helped get JFK elected!

Nixon said all the right words, but Kennedy said his words better. He said them in a way that conveyed the emotions behind his words. **Influence is the transference of emotion!** You primarily transfer emotion with body language. Let's take a look at some recent presidential elections. Set your political affiliation on the shelf for a minute. Which one of the following pairs did the best job of transferring emotion during the election process?

- Bill Clinton or Bob Dole

- Bill Clinton or George Bush

- Michael Dukakis or George Bush

- Walter Mondale or Ronald Reagan

Most people answer Clinton, Clinton (didn't George lose his emotional edge the second time around?), Bush, and Reagan. People vote for candidates who can move them emotionally. When it comes to influence, people are "voting" for you or your "competition." Learn to be good at attracting votes. "Turn up the volume" on your voice qualities and body language at least 20%. Believe in your PISA and convey that belief with an extra dose of emotion! The results will amaze you, and you'll enjoy the influence process so much more.

When you effectively influence someone, you guide them to **mentally** "buy into" your PISA. You now have an obligation to give it to them **physically**. You must follow through on your promise. When you do that, you will have repeat customers and numerous referrals. You will be rich financially and, more important, emotionally, because you have mastered the art of Elegant Influence.

Wow, we covered more material in this chapter than I anticipated when I planned this book. I tend to get carried away with the topic of influence because I believe it is such a vital skill for **everyone.** If you're in sales, your career depends on it. When you think about it, we're all in sales. If you're a parent, I hope you're a better salesperson than the people selling drugs on the street corner. If you're a leader of any group, large or small, I hope that you're a pro at influencing people to take action in ways where everyone wins. If you provide a service of any kind to internal or external customers, you're an influencer who will determine if the external customer stays with your company or the internal customer wants to stay in your relationship.

The Exercises for Action are especially important because the skills I discussed in this chapter are new to most people. Don't let these skills wilt on the vine. Pick them now and take a big bite by putting them into action in one or more of your relationships.

EXERCISES FOR ACTION

Record your answers in your journal or notebook.

1. Think of one influence relationship you have in your **personal** life. Discover the person's Values and Sparks. How can you use the Value Links discussed in this chapter to elegantly influence the person to take action?

2. Think of one influence relationship you have in your **business** life. Discover the person's Values and Sparks. How can you use the Value Links discussed in this chapter to elegantly influence the person to take action?

3. Think of a role you have where owning a toolbox full of Value Links would be extremely valuable. Create your personal toolbox with Value Links from the six groups.

4. Audiotape or videotape yourself in an influence situation. View the tape. How can you improve your voice qualities and body language to enhance the quality of your communication?

The Power of Giving

I n the last chapter, you learned the Foundational Rule of Giving: Give to others in ways that create a better long-term life for them. Give to others in ways that are in their best long-term interest. In this chapter, I hope you will come to more fully appreciate the immense power that is released when a gift is given and received.

That power is increased as you move down the four levels of giving as outlined on the next page.

The Four Levels of Giving

1. Level One—The receiver loses, and the giver wins. The giver is a *con artist*.

2. Level Two—The receiver wins, and the giver loses. The giver is a *martyr*.

3. Level Three—The receiver wins, and the giver wins. The giver is a *true friend*.

4. Level Four—The receiver wins, the giver wins, and other people win. The giver is a *team player*.

Level One—The receiver loses, and the giver wins. The giver is a *con artist*.

In reality, Level One isn't giving at all. It's taking under the guise of giving. All con artists take advantage of people by pretending to be givers. This can be done intentionally or unintentionally, but the result is the same.

Here is an example of unintentional Level One giving. Some financially rich parents give large sums of money to their children when they're young. This makes the parents feel like winners because they think it says, "We'll do everything we can to help the kids." But does the gift truly help the children in the long run? Usually not, because it robs them of their incentive to learn, grow, and work hard for their own success. The kids become complacent, thinking, *We've got it made. We don't have to work.*

Here's an example of intentional Level One giving. Some people don't feel good about themselves, and to make themselves feel better, they give other people the "gift" of put-downs and criticism. If accepted, those gifts tear other people down.

Likewise, con artists build themselves up by tearing others down—deliberately and often with an elaborate plan. Usually, they are exposed sooner or later. When this happens, they move on to a new "victim." Con artists seem to be winning in the short haul; they always lose in the end, however.

Are there any areas of your life where you are unconsciously being a Level One giver? The feeling of guilt is a signal that this is happening. Or other people may tell you that your "gift" doesn't feel like a gift. Remember, just because you *think* you're a giver, that doesn't mean you *are* one. The receiver is the final authority of what is truly a gift.

Level Two—The receiver wins, and the giver loses. The giver is a *martyr*.

Level Two is probably an improvement over Level One. The giver truly helps the other person, but gives so much or gives in such inappropriate ways that he/she is hurt in the long run. This may seem admirable, but martyr-like giving decreases the ability to give in the future, because there is little left to give.

Sometimes parents who work outside the home fall into this category. They give to their spouses. They give to their children.

They give to their employer. They give to their organizations. They give to their community. Then, at the end of the day, there is no time or energy left for themselves. They don't take care of themselves physically, emotionally, or spiritually, which can lead to burnout or the "Is this all there is?" syndrome. The best thing these people can do is to pull back on some of their giving so they have the ability to keep on giving in the long run.

You also may want to examine your life for any instances of Level Two giving. A sure sign of this is feeling unfulfilled after you give. I had this happen in my life about a year ago. As a speaker, trainer, and consultant, I'm asked on numerous occasions to give free presentations to not-for-profit groups such as Head Start, Job Corps, schools, prisons, and civic groups. I was doing about twenty of these presentations a year. I love giving to these groups, but on a long plane ride home from one of these presentations, I was feeling resentful about it. I'd been away from my family too much, and I didn't feel good about that. I wasn't making much progress with this book, and I was frustrated with that.

So I made the decision to limit myself to eight free presentations each year. Three of them had to be in the San Diego area where I live. My decision has worked out well. I'm much more discriminating about who I do presentations for, and I feel good about each one I do. There will probably be a time in my life when I will want to increase the number, but for now eight per year is the right number for me.

Level Three—The receiver wins, and the giver wins. The giver is a *true friend*.

In Level Three, there are no losers. The giver and receiver both benefit. This book is full of examples of Level Three giving. When I take Belinda to the Family Fun Center, that's Level Three giving. When I provide excellent service to a client, that's Level Three giving.

With Level Three giving, both parties benefit because the act of giving provides energy to a series of events I call the Cycle of Life. The Cycle of Life is described in detail below. To make it more personal, let's make you the giver.

The Cycle of Life

The Cycle of Life has four stages: BE, DO, HAVE, and GIVE. BEing is where it all begins—when you are BEing resourceful, happy, or loving, for example, you will DO resourceful, happy, or loving things.

DO is the second stage of the Cycle of Life. Much of our lives is spent doing things, but we have to ask ourselves whether we're doing the things that are meaningful, that will make a difference for ourselves and others. If your actions, your DOing, arise from empowering states of BEing, you will naturally choose to DO what is meaningful and important. I also believe that there is a higher power that will give you the power to run your Cycle of Life. It's vital that you tap into this power source on a regular basis.

HAVE is the third stage of the Cycle of Life. Most people focus almost exclusively on the HAVE stage, and forget they have to BE and DO first! When you consistently DO the right things, you will HAVE the things you desire in life. You will HAVE all the relationships, emotions, and possessions that accompany a life well lived.

Now that you HAVE what you desire, you can't stop there—you must move to the fourth stage of the cycle. You must GIVE from what you HAVE. And more important than giving anything material, you must GIVE to others your positive emotional states, like happiness, and love. You must GIVE away your support and knowledge. And yes, when appropriate, you may choose to GIVE your physical assets as well. Your goal in giving should always be to enable the recipients to BE more in their own lives. When the giving is done precisely because you have accurately discovered the other person's Values and Sparks, you are truly practicing the Diamond Touch.

Giving is a vital part of the Cycle of Life for two reasons. First, you will receive from life that which you give. When you give support, happiness, and love, for example, you will receive support, happiness, and love in your life because you will attract people and experiences that will enhance these positive emotions inside you. When you reflect a resourceful attitude to the world, you will attract the very resources you need—whether they be physical, emotional, or spiritual—that will move you toward your personal vision. When you give happiness, you will attract it; when you give love, you become a magnet for all the love in the world. And these gifts of life will enhance your BEing, and the Cycle of Life can begin anew with even greater power!

Second, when you acquire the Diamond Touch and GIVE to others in empowering ways, they will never BE the same. You will help enhance their BEing, and a new improved Cycle of Life will begin for them, allowing them to DO and HAVE more—and GIVE more to others as well. Your Cycles of Life become connected. It looks like this:

The Interdependent Cycles of Life

Level Four—The receiver wins, the giver wins, and other people win. The giver is a *team player*.

Level Four is the highest level at which you can play the giving game. At Level Four, the receiver wins, you win, and other people win. This is nothing more than connecting numerous Cycles of Life together to create one ever-expanding Upward Spiral of Life.

The Upward Spiral of Life

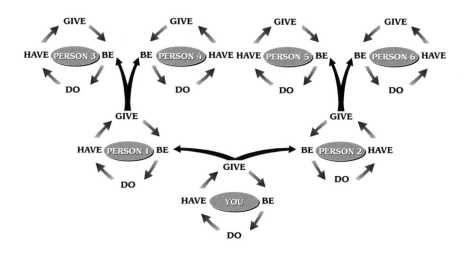

Here's a simple yet revealing example of creating an Upward Spiral of Life. As part of my travels, I take taxis in most cities I visit. I have two basic choices when I'm in the cab. I can ignore the driver and stay in my own world. Or I can have a meaningful conversation with the driver and learn from his experience—which is almost always vastly different from my own. During the conversation I can always give the driver the gift of respect and appreciation. I ask about his or her experiences in life (often experiences gained in a different country). I ask for opinions of our country and us as a people. I ask, "What's one thing we Americans could learn from the people in your native country?"

At the end of the ride, I always give a nice tip, and just as important, I look the driver in the eye, shake hands, and say, "I appreciate the great service and the information you gave me." If they act interested in what I'm doing, I like to give drivers a copy of one of my books.

This is Level Four giving because:

1. The other person wins by receiving the gifts of respect and appreciation that enhance BEing.

2. I win. I enjoy seeing drivers come alive as they talk with me. You should see the change in their faces from the beginning to the end of the ride.

3. Do you think it stops here? How do drivers treat the next person in the cab? Perhaps a little bit better. How do they treat their families when they go home? Perhaps a little bit better. Maybe they'll even read the book to gain some knowledge that will make their lives and the lives of the people they care about better. In short, other people will win as a result of my gift.

When it comes to Level Four giving, you might be thinking, *But there is so much I want to do. Where do I start?* Start with yourself. As Mahatma Gandhi said, "We must become the change we seek in the world." Create a BEing who has enormous spiritual, emotional, physical, and even financial riches. Then create an attitude of giving. Look for places in all areas of your life where you can give at Levels Three and Four.

After you have created your personal treasure chest of gifts, begin giving to those closest to you—your spouse, your children, your parents, and your siblings. Bob and Elizabeth Dole and the Republicans were right in the 1996 presidential campaign. As they said often, "It takes a family." The most precious gifts of all are the ones given to your family.

After you have given to your family, you can begin to give to those in your community. Hillary and Bill Clinton and the Democrats were right in the 1996 presidential campaign when they said, "It takes a village." Are there people in your village who could benefit from your gifts of time, attention, and resources? If so, give to them on a regular basis. It's up to you how big you want to make your village—how many Cycles of Life you want to affect. As our world gets smaller, our community gets bigger. Our challenges and opportunities increase.

There's another piece of the puzzle that we need to explore. For every giver, there is a receiver. How good are you at receiving? Do you make it easy for others to jump-start their Cycle of Life by giving to you? If you don't, you're being selfish.

A few years ago, I noticed that I was not fully accepting people's compliments. They would give me praise for a presentation, and I would get embarrassed, look away, and say, "Oh, I don't know about that," or "You probably say that to everybody." Then I began thinking, *Who wins when I say that?* Nobody wins. I was being selfish. Now, when people give me a compliment, I look them right in the eye and say, "Thank you. I really appreciate you saying that!" They win. I win. Everyone's Cycle of Life flows a little faster.

When it comes right down to it, life is the flow of energy. When energy stops flowing in an organism or an organization, it dies. Giving is the passing of energy. Receiving is the acceptance of energy. Both are needed for the energy circuit to be complete.

I hope this book, *The Diamond Touch,* will enable you to take your level of giving and receiving to a higher level. Then the energy circuits in your life will flow with ease, creating deep relationships that prosper and endure. After all, a diamond is forever.

ABOUT THE AUTHOR

For over 30 years, Dr. Nate Booth has been relentlessly studying, applying, and coaching others in the art of thriving in times of rapid change. Nate received his DDS degree from the University of Nebraska in 1971 and was in private dental practice for eight years. In 1983, he decided to switch careers and earned a master's degree in counseling.

His company, Nate Booth & Associates, creates customized training programs for corporations and associations around the world. Clients include Aetna, AIG, American Dental Association, AT&T, Blue Cross–Blue Shield, Century 21, Eastman Kodak, Honeywell, IBM, *Inc.* Magazine, Kraft Foods, Mobil Oil, NASA, Norwest Bank, Northwestern Mutual Life, Prudential Insurance, Sanyo, Saturn Corporation, Siemens Corporation, University of California Irvine School of Medicine, University of South Carolina School of Business, Midwest Gas Association, and the National Auto Dealers Association.

Nate has three children—Chris, Emily, and Belinda—and he currently resides in Las Vegas, Nevada.

Dr. Booth would love to hear from you! Please send your success stories in using *The Diamond Touch* to him by e-mail at nbooth@natebooth.com, by fax to (702)444-0762, or by mail to

Nate Booth & Associates

1365 Fox Acres Drive

Las Vegas, NV 89134

OTHER NATE BOOTH PRODUCTS

THRIVING ON CHANGE
The Art of Using Change to Your Advantage

Rapid and never-ending change is a fact of life in today's world. What isn't a fact yet is how all this change is going to affect you! Some people live life at the mercy of change and avoid it at all costs. Others try to cope with change and just "hang in there." Change Masters are a different breed. They thrive on change! They know that rapid change levels the playing field and creates tremendous opportunities for anyone who knows the new rules of the game. In short, Change Masters use change to their advantage in their personal lives and businesses! In this refreshing and interactive book, you will learn the change utilization skills needed to create the future you desire and deserve.

"Thriving on Change will help you create a magnificent future and lifestyle—for yourself, those you love, and our world. It's full of brilliant, thought-provoking insight."

MARK VICTOR HANSEN
Co-author, the *Chicken Soup for the Soul* series of books

"When you read this book, you will immediately be able to thrive on the constant change around you. Dr. Booth has packed Thriving on Change *with dozens of practical methods you can use tomorrow to improve your life!"*

KEN DYCHWALD, PH.D.
Author, *Age Wave*

333-page hardcover book, $24.95

Quantity Discounts Are Available on All Products.
Please call us at 800-917-0008 or visit our website at www.natebooth.com.

JUMP-START YOUR DAY

Each day you probably spend 15 to 40 minutes on your appearance so you can look good on the outside. How much time do you spend preparing emotionally so you can feel good on the inside? Most people answer, "Zero." *Jump-Start Your Day* will help you change that. On the first audiocassette, you will learn how to use your mental and physical pathways to consistently produce resourceful emotions. The second audiocassette is divided into six segments: Monday, Tuesday, and Wednesday on Side A and Thursday, Friday, and Saturday/Sunday on Side B. As you listen to one eight-minute segment each morning, you will create the energy and enthusiasm you need to fly through the day with passion and purpose!

2 Audiocassettes, $24.95

Quantity Discounts Are Available on All Products.
Please call us at 800-917-0008 or visit our website at www.natebooth.com.

THE INFLUENCE FACTOR
How to Create Change in Yourself and Others

You can be the most knowledgeable and caring person in the world, with the best ideas and intentions, but your impact will be severely limited if you can't influence other people and yourself to take action. The world is changing rapidly around you. The Influence Factor—your ability to create change in yourself and others—is a skill you must possess in order to keep up with this external change. Most influence programs are a collection of techniques that you "lay on" people. **The Influence Factor** is different. You will learn psychological reasons behind why people choose to take action, so that you can naturally enter the process and elegantly influence others and yourself to change for the better.

Here are a few of the dynamic and impactful strategies you will learn:

1. How to create an identity and reputation that inspires you and influences others.

2. How to quickly create trust and rapport with anyone you meet.

3. Three elegant ways to transfer emotion so that people want to take action.

4. How to quickly discover what emotions people really want in their lives and what has to happen for them to experience the emotions. Now you can influence them

to action by showing them how they can get what they want with your idea, product, service, or action.

5. How to weld Value Links between what people really want and the change you want them to make.

6. How to ask Triple Impact Questions to get the information you need to understand what "makes people tick."

7. How to create urgency so that other people and you want to take action now!

8. How to use **The Influence Factor** in all the important relationships of your life—husband/wife, parent/child, friendships, colleague/co-worker, influence relationships, and service relationships.

9. How to create change in yourself by creating a compelling vision that inspires you to naturally "do the right thing."

10. How each of the BE, DO, HAVE, and GIVE parts of your Cycle of Life can be used to "jump-start" the other parts of the cycle to create a flow of energy that powers you to your life goals!

The Influence Factor is a powerful set of skills that will enjoyably enable you to create the change in others and yourself to create the world you desire and deserve!

6 Audiocassettes and Learner's Guide, $59.95

Quantity Discounts Are Available on All Products.
Please call us at 800-917-0008 or visit our website at www.natebooth.com.

ELEGANT INFLUENCE FOR DENTISTS

The Art of Influencing Your Patients to Say "Yes!"

Would you like to provide more high quality dentistry to your patients? Most dentists answer with a resounding "Yes!" Does high quality dentistry "sell" itself? Most dentists answer with a disappointing "No." In order to increase your level of case acceptance, you and your staff will need to master the art of elegantly influencing patients to say "Yes!" When this happens, your patients will receive the treatment they deserve and your office will achieve the practice goals you desire.

Because influence is the entire office's responsibility, **Elegant Influence for Dentists** is designed to be studied in ten office staff meetings. In the privacy of your office, you will learn the communication secrets of the world's best influencers.

Here are a few of the dynamic and impactful communication strategies your team will learn:

- How to take fear out of influence so that the patient and you feel comfortable with the process.

- How to naturally enter the patient's decision making process to help the person choose optimal dental health.

- How to create a reputation that sets the stage for easy acceptance of your treatment plans.

- How to gain trust and rapport with any patient.

- How to discover the unique "buying motives" of each patient.

- How to use "Value Links" to connect the patient's "buying motives" with your treatment plan.

- How to avoid the three communication errors that lead to case refusal.

- How to move patients from "I want to think about it" to "Let's get started!"

- How to elegantly ask patients to "open a relationship" instead of "close a sale."

- How to make the case presentation appointment an enjoyable and learning experience for everyone!

The **Elegant Influence** office study program contains eight audiocassette tapes, five 93-page Learner's Guides (one for each staff member), and a Leader's Guide. In ten action-packed staff meetings, you will listen to Nate Booth, DDS and Brenda Kaesler, RDH present the Seven Steps to Elegant Influence. The true power of the program comes next. Each staff meeting concludes with an Exercises for Action section where your team will practice the skills and develop a plan for using the skills in your unique office situation.

8 Audiocassettes, 5 Learner's Guides, and a Leader's Guide, $295.00

Quantity Discounts Are Available on All Products.
Please call us at 800-917-0008 or visit our website at www.natebooth.com.

NATE BOOTH & ASSOCIATES CORPORATE AND ASSOCIATION TRAINING PROGRAMS

Invite Nate Booth & Associates to your corporation or association for a high-energy keynote presentation; an impactful half- or full-day workshop; or a comprehensive multi-day training program. Each topic can be customized for general audiences, salespeople, leaders, or managers. The staff of Nate Booth & Associates is also available on a consulting basis to enhance your personal or your group's performance in the rapidly changing business world.

THE DIAMOND TOUCH PROGRAMS

We're all familiar with the Golden Rule: "Treat people the way you would like to be treated." The Golden Rule is a powerful principle, but it has one shortcoming. Everyone wants to be treated differently. If you're a service provider, people want to be served differently. If you're a salesperson, people want to be influenced differently. If you're a leader, people want to be led differently.

This variety of desires is what makes relationships interesting and challenging. It's also the reason why you can't take a cookie-cutter approach to service, influence, or leadership in today's diverse and ever-changing world. The good news is this variety of desires creates tremendous opportunities for those companies and people who understand and practice the Diamond Rule. The Diamond Rule is, "Treat others in the unique way they want to be treated." Those who have the Diamond Touch quickly and precisely discover the unique desires of their internal and external customers. Then, whenever possible, they give them what they want, in the way they want it, to create close relationships that last.

Here are a few of the dynamic and impactful strategies your team will learn:

- Why a "one size fits all" relationship philosophy is doomed to fail in our highly individualized world.

- The two questions you must ask to quickly discover what people want and how they want it.

- How to quickly create trust and rapport with almost anyone you meet.

- How to use the Five Lifestyle Groups as a guide to applying the Diamond Touch.

- The four costly mistakes most people make when dealing with customers.

- Three 60-Second Strategies for dealing with difficult people.

THE DIAMOND TOUCH

In this program, designed for general audiences, you will enjoyably learn how to make the Diamond Rule a way of life in all your most important relationships!

DIAMOND TOUCH SERVICE

In this program designed for service providers, you will learn how to give the customized service that will keep people coming back again and again!

DIAMOND TOUCH INFLUENCE

In this program designed for salespeople, you will learn how to influence people to want to take action according to their unique set of Values and Sparks!

DIAMOND TOUCH LEADERSHIP

In this program designed for leaders, you will learn how to lead each member of your team according to their unique set of Values and Sparks!

To learn more about any of these programs,
call 800-917-0008 or visit our website at www.natebooth.com.

CHANGE MASTERY PROGRAMS

THRIVING ON CHANGE
The Art of Using Change to Your Advantage

Rapid and never-ending change is a fact in today's world. What isn't a fact is how all this change is going to affect your company and you! Some corporations and people live at the mercy of change and avoid it at all costs. Others try to cope with change and just "hang in there." But Change Masters are a different breed. They thrive on change! They know that rapid change creates tremendous opportunities for those who know the new rules of the game.

In changing times, the same set of beliefs and strategies that have gotten you to where you are now will not get you to where you want to go. When things change, you must change. The thrill of running a company or living a life is knowing what to change, what to keep, and when and how to do each. In **Thriving on Change,** your group will learn the skills needed to use any change to their advantage, creating greater success on all levels. This program can be customized for general audiences, leaders, managers, or salespeople, and scheduled in keynote, half-day, full-day, or two-day formats.

Here are a few of the dynamic and impactful strategies your group will learn:

- The power of principles, and the habits they create, to shape your corporate culture and your life.

- The Six Thriving on Change Beliefs. These beliefs are the foundation of all successful change utilization.

- The success strategies corporations and individuals use to harness the tremendous power of change.

- The Four Change Utilization Questions you need to ask yourself to transform every change into an opportunity.

- The Three Keys to Anticipating Change.

- The Seven Steps to Creating Change.

- How you and your company can continually learn and grow so that you are smart, quick, and flexible enough to consistently use change to your advantage!

Thriving on Change is an enjoyable, interactive, and results-oriented program that will inspire your people to tap their unlimited potential in changing times!

To learn more about any of these programs,
call 800-917-0008 or visit our website at www.natebooth.com.

LEGENDARY LEADERSHIP
In Times of Rapid Change

Constant change is a fact of life in today's business world. When external circumstances are changing rapidly, effective leaders are more important than ever. Some groups are weakened when change occurs; others welcome the changing environment and use it as a time to learn, create, grow, and contribute more. In **Legendary Leadership,** your group will learn the essential beliefs and skills outstanding leaders employ to create an environment where change brings out the very best in people! You can schedule the program in keynote, half-day, or full-day formats.

Here are a few of the dynamic and impactful strategies your group will learn:

- The core beliefs of the most successful leaders in the world: the foundation upon which all action is based.

- The success strategies of leaders who have learned to harness the power of change to their advantage.

- Four Change Utilization Questions that can transform every change into an opportunity.

- The four mistakes most leaders make when dealing with change.

- How to keep your group motivated in the midst of rapid change.

- How to lead people through the Three Steps of Successful Change: 1) Letting Go of the Old; 2) Transitioning between the Old and the New; 3) Embracing the New.

- How to correctly anticipate change so you can help your team prepare for it.

The ***Legendary Leadership*** program will give your leaders the tools they need to create an environment where change is welcomed as the spark for group and personal improvement.

To learn more about any of these programs,
call 800-917-0008 or visit our website at www.natebooth.com.

MOTIVATIONAL PROGRAMS

THE RACE FOR THE FUTURE BEGINS TODAY

The race for the future begins today! The race will be won by those who are the smartest, quickest, and most flexible—those who are prepared for the challenge and emotionally "fit" for the journey. *The Race for the Future Begins Today* will give your group the inspiration to approach the starting line with eagerness, the skills to enjoyably and effectively run the race, and the vision to "break the tape" at the finish line and create the future they desire and deserve. You can schedule the program in keynote, half-day, or full-day formats.

Here are a few of the dynamic and impactful strategies your group will learn:

- How to create a compelling vision of the future that will inspire you to make it a reality!

- How to create a solid foundation for your life based on universal principles.

- How to use the three keys to race effectively for the future: Be smart. Be flexible. Be quick.

- How to keep yourself and your team in peak, powerful, and resourceful emotional states on a consistent basis.

- How to improve using innovation and plussing so you're always one step ahead of the game.

- How to enjoyably "juggle more balls" than ever before.

- How to create a continuous BE - DO - HAVE - GIVE CYCLE that will spiral you and the people you care about upwards to the future you desire!

The Race for the Future Begins Today is an inspirational, interactive and results-oriented program that will give your group the tools they need to win the race to the future!

To learn more about any of these programs,
call 800-917-0008 or visit our website at www.natebooth.com.

DREAM QUEST

They all had a dream! John F. Kennedy didn't hope to explore space. He created a national dream to "put a man on the moon and bring him back alive before the end of the decade." Mary Kay Ash didn't want to build a company that sold cosmetics. She envisioned a company that would "give women the opportunity to do anything they were smart enough to do." Walt Disney didn't want to make cartoons for kids. His dream was to "use imagination to bring happiness to millions!" **Big results are the creation of Big Dreams, and you and your team deserve both!** Using inspiring stories and compelling videotape segments, and with practical strategies your group can use immediately, the *Dream Quest* program will crystallize the five steps visionaries use to make their dreams come true. This program can be scheduled in keynote, half-day, full-day, or two-day formats.

In the *Dream Quest* program, your group will learn The Five Steps to Making Dreams Come True:

Step 1. *Have a Crystal Clear and Inspiring Dream.* You've got to have a dream to make a dream come true! An inspiring dream is the catalyst that mobilizes the resources for its achievement.

Step 2. *Believe that You Can Live Your Dream.* When it comes to living your dream, you'll see it when you believe it.

Step 3. ***Enthusiastically and Intelligently Move toward Your Dream.*** People who are excited but don't know what they are doing are dangerous! Be confident and competent as you move toward your dream.

Step 4. ***Embrace Challenges Along the Way.*** Challenges are the events you run into that remind you of your progress. The bigger the dream, the bigger the challenges will probably be!

Step 5. ***Realize that the Journey is the Reward.*** As strange as it seems, achieving your dream is not what's most important. Who you become as a person on the way to your dream—and what your company becomes on the way to its dream—that's what's truly important!

We all need a dream to make a dream come true. **Dream Quest** will provide the inspiration and skills you and your team will need to turn dreams into realities.

To learn more about any of these programs,
call 800-917-0008 or visit our website at www.natebooth.com.

LIFE BALANCE

The daily demands on your time and attention are unending. Work, family, and personal time are all clamoring for your immediate attention. Congratulations: you're intensely wanted! The challenge lies in allocating the appropriate time and attention to each area of your life. The **Life Balance** program will show you how to enjoyably get the right things done. Then, at the end of a day, you'll feel the rewards of a life that's not just busy, but well lived! You can schedule this program in keynote, half-day, full-day, or two-day formats.

In the **Life Balance** program your group will learn how to:

- Crystallize what is truly important to you in your life.

- Consistently do the things that are important, not just urgent.

- Create balance and synergy among the various roles in your life.

- Jump off the "harder/faster/more" treadmill.

- Set and achieve balanced goals that produce quality results.

- Create a weekly guide that will assist you in enjoyably accomplishing the important goals of your life.

- Break the vicious cycle of procrastination and crisis.

- Make time for renewal of body, mind, and spirit.

- Turn your days into an upward spiral of living and learning.

If you ever hear people in your group say, "There just aren't enough hours in the day!" or "There's not enough of me to go around!" then the **Life Balance** program is for you. It will give your group the essential skills needed to create lives that are more productive and rewarding.

To learn more about any of these programs,
call 800-917-0008 or visit our website at www.natebooth.com.

INFLUENCE BEGINS WITH "I"

The most important "sale" you will ever make is the one before you meet your customer/client! Influence is the transference of emotion, and you can't give something away that you don't have. To influence other people, you must first be influenced! In **Influence Begins with "I,"** your group will learn how to create the beliefs, emotions, and presence that will consistently and effectively influence your customers/clients to take action! You can schedule the program in keynote, half-day, or full-day formats.

Here are a few of the impactful and dynamic strategies your group will learn:

- The psychological principles behind why people take action so you can enter the process naturally.

- How to "connect" with people instantly.

- Three tools all effective communicators use to create emotion.

- How to create an identity and reputation that inspires you and influences others. What your customers/clients know about you before they meet you is vital to your success!

- How to construct a solid personal foundation that will provide a base for win-win interaction.

- How to truly enjoy the influence process.

The *Influence Begins with "I"* program is unique. It is loaded with tools and strategies that will improve your people's influence skills and your bottom line.

To learn more about any of these programs,
call 800-917-0008 or visit our website at www.natebooth.com.

♦ 267

BUSTING THROUGH YOUR BARRIERS

People want to grow and succeed. They want to move beyond their current boundaries and limitations, achieve their dreams, and contribute more to their corporations and all the teams of their lives! There is one thing that stands in the way, however. Fear—fear of failure, fear of the unknown, fear of standing out in a group, even fear of success. **Busting Through Your Barriers** will show your team how to bust through self-imposed barriers by giving them the experience of breaking through a wooden board karate-style—a feat most people don't believe they can do! As thousands of people can attest, this experience is worth a million words. The half- or full-day **Busting Through Your Barriers** program will educate, entertain, and inspire your group so they will leave with the confidence and competence to break through other barriers in their lives!

Here are a few of the dynamic and impactful strategies your group will learn:

- The Four Keys to Effective Barrier Busting: empowering beliefs, effective strategies, peak emotional states, and a supportive team.

- Why you need to be confident and competent to bust through a barrier.

- How to use modeling to quickly reproduce excellence in any area of life.

- How to play on a team where people support each other so that everyone learns and grows.

- How to use all that you have learned during the day to safely and enjoyably break a wooden board at the end of the program. The energy, synergy, and commitment generated in the room is incredible!

Busting Through Your Barriers is not like any training program your team has ever experienced. It will set your entire team *on fire* to achieve both their personal goals and your corporate objectives!

To learn more about any of these programs,
call 800-917-0008 or visit our website at www.natebooth.com.

Here's what people are saying about Nate Booth & Associates' corporate and association training programs:

"Congratulations! You were rated number one out of fifty speakers at Inc. *magazine's Fifth Annual Conference on Customer Service. Tremendous job!"*

KEVIN GILLIGAN
Conference Producer
Inc. Magazine

"I have seen motivational presentations on topics before, but in my opinion, your enthusiasm and technique are second to none!"

ANN KROUPA
Vice President, Specialized Markets
AT&T

"In my twenty-five years as a conference organizer, I have never seen a speaker achieve perfect marks from an audience—until you came along!"

JIM COULSON
Director of Education
University of California Irvine Medical Center

"Little did I believe you could keep our high-energy group contained and excited for a full four hours. Yet your material, coupled with your delivery style of speed, wit, and participation, kept all two hundred riveted and involved."

DICK MORGAN
Director of Marketing
Milgard Windows

"Congratulations on being rated number one out of twenty speakers at our recent convention. I heard nothing but wonderful comments about your program!"

KATHI BROWN
Workshop Coordinator
National Automobile Dealers Association

"Thank you for delivering such an informative and entertaining opening session and subsequent presentations at our Dallas Winter Show in January. They were rated the highest out of 42 workshops we offered that day!"

NANCI KINDLE
Administrator, Continuing
Education Programs
Specialty Advertising Association
International

"You did it again: You received exceptional marks throughout all the evaluations. You are truly the best speaker I have ever heard. Our members are constantly singing your praises and asking for more of Dr. Nate Booth."

CARMELA PORTER
Executive Director
Professional Association of
Health Care Office Managers

". . . This was the first time that Scitor had made use of an outside speaker at any of our company meetings. It was a risk—but as the attached subset of comments extracted from our internal survey of attending employees indicate, it was a total success! Just so you understand the top-level feedback of our employees, 97% of those returning their surveys stated that your segment 'Exceeded Expectations.'"

TERRY PETRZELKA
President
Scitor Corporation

"Outstanding. Your presentation to NTS senior management was timely, enthusiastic, and right on. Several attendees commented on your excellent delivery style and, most important, the action-oriented content of your presentation."

DIANA (SAM) INGRAHAM
Norwest Technical Services

"Thank you from the 300+ NML leadership team members who were challenged by you at our annual meeting. I have heard nothing but praise and excitement about your presentation content, delivery style, and just YOU!"

BARB JAMES, CLU, CHFC
Field Development Consultant
Northwestern Mutual Life

"Based on the audience evaluations your session received an average rating of 4.5 for content and a 4.7 for delivery, on a 5 point scale. These audience ratings show that you were the highest rated speaker at the conference. Congratulations!"

BRIAN S. COSTELLO
Conference Producer
International Business Communica-
tions

"Wow! What a great seminar! Our meeting critique reported that you were voted 'Best Speaker/Presenter' and listed the most when asked the question, 'Which presentation did you gain the most from?'"

THERESA KIRKLEY
Office Administrator
Choice Management & Realty Services

"As I sat in the audience, I couldn't help but feel the energy—not only from you—but from the participants as well. I know it takes a terrific amount of dedication and commitment to create the 'perfect' show—and this show was PERFECT! I cannot begin to tell you how much you have positively impacted so many employees through this one event! In fact, we have been inundated with notes and phone messages thanking us for your powerful presentation and message. It was not only timely, but absolutely needed considering our recent merger announcement."

MARY KOWALSKY
Vice President
Southwest Event Management
Bank of America

"Your topic and delivery were perfect. It is very difficult to keep the attention of an audience for two hours. You did, and you did so magnificently! As a matter of fact, we were so impressed we would like to have you again next year for our annual meeting in San Francisco."

STEPHEN A. RALLS, DDS, EdD, MSD
Executive Director
American College of Dentists